EQUAL TO THE CHALLENGE

EQUAL TO THE CHALLENGE

Pioneering Women of Horse Sports

Jackie C. Burke

HOWELL BOOK HOUSE
NEW YORK

Howell Book House
A Simon & Schuster Macmillan Company
1633 Broadway
New York, NY 10019

MACMILLAN is a registered trademark of Macmillan, Inc.

Library of Congress Cataloging-in-Publication Data
Burke, Jackie C.
     Equal to the challenge: pioneering women of horse sports / Jackie C. Burke.
          p.   cm.
     Includes bibliographical references (p. 191) and index.
     ISBN 0-87605-727-X
     1. Women in horse sports—History.   I. Title.
SF284.4.B87   1997
798'.082—dc21   97-1898
                                                                   CIP

Manufactured in the United States of America

10 9 8 7 6 5 4 3 2 1

for
my daughters
Betsy and Jennifer

Contents

Acknowledgments   *ix*

1. History Viewed with 20/20 Hindsight   *1*

2. Once Upon a Sidesaddle   *11*

3. Getting into the Game   *27*

4. Pioneers on the Backstretch   *45*

5. Dressage—A Perfect Sport for Women   *57*

6. Jumping to the Forefront, or The Only Flower Strong Enough   *75*

7. Eventing—Fearing the Worst, Achieving the Best   *101*

8. Women's Race Track Suffrage, or "This Isn't Going to Be a Problem"   *131*

9. Winning the Race Against the Male Establishment, or What Part Don't You Understand?   *143*

10. Steeplechasing—You'd Never Hear a Girl Say That   *161*

Epilog   *181*

Bibliography   *191*

Index   *195*

Acknowledgments

After writing a book, the author is tempted to offer a list of thank you's as long as that of a first-time Academy Award winner. It is enough to say that almost every person named in *Equal to the Challenge* who was alive when I was working on the book not only answered my phone calls, but also my endless questions, and for that I am grateful. Sources whose names do not appear—the families and associates of those already deceased or whom I could not find—also generously gave of their time. I will not attempt to list those in either category but must single out a few who went above and beyond the call of duty. Behind the scenes but indispensable were Laura Rose and Peter Winants of the National Sporting Library; they not only found sources I requested but also produced many pertinent articles I would have otherwise missed. Then there were experts in their fields who not only answered questions but also edited chapters to assure details were correct. These include George "Smokey" Everhart, Mrs. Nancy Hannum, Mrs. Jo Motion, Jessica Ransehousen, Marjorie Gill, William C. Steinkraus, Gen. Jonathan Burton, Sheila Willcox, and Diane Crump. Kathy Kusner read almost every chapter because, with her varied endeavors, she appears in almost every chapter.

Finally, thanks to a long list of family, friends, and neighbors who read copy and offered constructive criticism. I also bored my foxhunting friends with long-winded accounts of each detail unearthed by my research, and I know they share my joy that the project is finally complete.

1

History Viewed with 20/20 Hindsight

IN 1971, THE COMMITTEE OF THE MARYLAND HUNT CUP faced a difficult decision. Kathy Kusner, one of the best show jump riders of the day, wanted to ride in the legendary race. She was more than qualified—she had already represented the United States in the Olympics in 1964 and 1968 (and would again in 1972) and was twice Woman's World Show Jumping Champion. But she was, after all, a woman.

The committee had a dilemma. It had always been understood that the Maryland Hunt Cup was open to "gentlemen riders." She obviously didn't fit this classification.

Furthermore, the gentle, conservative patricians on the Hunt Cup Committee were genuinely concerned. The Maryland Hunt Cup course is, with England's Grand National Steeplechase, the most difficult in the world. On average, just over half the entries finish the race. The falls over the solid timber fences, which stand up to five feet three inches in height, are spectacular, and injuries are occasionally sustained. What if Kusner fell—worse, what if she were injured? Male participants fell all the time, but Charles Fenwick Sr., secretary of the meet, said, "Everyone would say, "Of course she was hurt. She's only a woman, and the committee should not have permitted her to ride."

Three-time Olympian Kathy Kusner (here with her 1964 and 1968 Olympic mount Untouchable) was almost barred from riding in the Maryland Hunt Cup because she was a woman. Photo: Courtesy of Kathy Kusner.

When this story and others of women's travails breaking into the Olympics, steeplechases, and flat racing were shared at Pony Club Camp in the summer of 1994, the young audience found it hard to understand why permitting women to ride was such a big deal.

"Well," I tried to explain, "women were just considered too weak and frail for such demanding and dangerous sports." This answer left the group even more incredulous. "Why did they think women were weak"? asked one truly perplexed eight-year-old girl.

The definition comes straight from the dictionary, which lists one of the definitions of *woman* as a derogatory term applied to men with characteristics regarded as feminine, such as weakness, timidity, inclination to gossip, etc. *Feminine, Webster's* tells us, is having qualities regarded as characteristic of a woman, such as gentleness, weakness, delicacy, modesty, and so on. *Womanish* means effeminate, emasculated, cowardly, shrill, vixenish, soft, weak. *Female,* in *Roget's College Thesaurus,* is the fair sex, weaker sex, or frail. St. Paul referred to women as the weaker vessel, and Shakespeare adopted the metaphor.

Considering these definitions, it's not that hard to see where the idea of women's athletic prowess, or lack of it, originated. Add to that the attitude of the Victorian Age, when men took on a particularly protective attitude toward women, determined to keep them from harm or hardship. During that era, athletic pursuits considered appropriate for women were pretty much limited to croquet.

Perhaps I should have told the Pony Clubbers that as late as the 1960s, men still made the decisions, and that most women just didn't question the way things were.

This is the story of women who not only questioned such decisions, but also acted on their beliefs.

Included in this book are tales of the early successes women achieved once they won the right to compete. You may not find stories about your own favorite rider because this book focuses on the first to compete and the first to win, and does not set out to make subjective judgments on the most worthy of the many worthy equestriennes. To learn more about great women riders, check the bibliography. The sources listed will provide more information about the individuals in this book, along with general histories that give a good view of the status of women during the Middle Ages and through eighteenth-century England right up to present-day America. Of course, now we can watch great women riders at any horse event and read of their latest triumphs in magazines and newspapers.

I grew up watching the changes elaborated on in this book, but didn't understand what I was seeing until Charles Fenwick Sr. described his

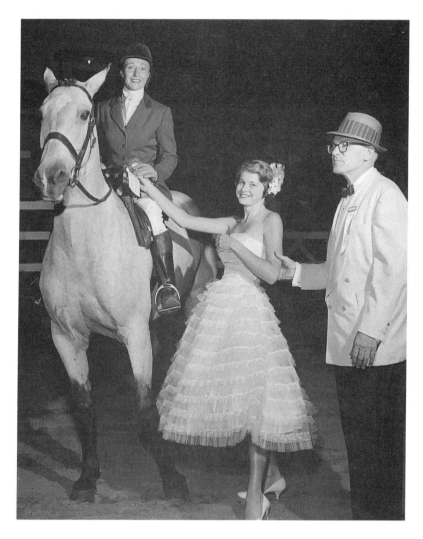

Joan Morganthau, master of the Branchwater Hunt, won horse shows all over the South-east with her great champion Copan. Ribbon presenter Becky Dial, a classmate of the author, displays proper apparel for young ladies of the day. Photo: Lewis Arnold, Sun Photo Service; courtesy of Pat Thuss.

concern about Kathy Kusner's ride in the Hunt Cup. I thought to myself, "that was such a short time ago, and the world has changed so much since then."

Before 1970, women thought differently. For example, when I was in the seventh grade in the 1950s, and as skinny as a stick, I tugged on my first girdle, a miserable tight elastic contraption that women wore as a right of passage and to hold up their stockings before some genius invented panty hose. At the small liberal arts college in the Deep South I attended in the 1960s, women were not permitted to wear slacks of any sort on campus, except on Saturdays, and then only if covered by a long coat. (Men wanted to leave no doubt about who wore the pants in the family.) When I continued wearing my raincoat over my riding clothes the summer I attended a larger university further north, I was often asked if it was raining. It never occurred to me that women could wear pants on campus.

No matter what the rules regarding equestrian competition were, I always knew that women could ride just as well as men. That was obvious from my first riding lesson, though none of us could keep pace with classmate Dennis Murphy, who went on to represent the United States in the jumping event at the 1976 Olympics. Mignon C. Smith owned Mede Cahaba, the riding school where I took lessons once a week, and Joan Morganthau was master of the local hunt. I thrilled to watch these two, along with Penny Robinson (later Johnson), Pat Thuss, and other women, dominate local horse shows. I cannot think back on those days and name a single man who so impressed me, except Murphy, who remains a friend and whose career I follow, and Col. Howard Morris, one of the early dressage virtuosos and first presidents of the U.S. Pony Club.

During my grammar school days, I began to read everything about horses that I could find in the school library. There was *National Velvet,* of course, and other books that are today less memorable. The prevalent theme in all of these involved a young woman's love for her horse, and how the two overcame difficulties to win the Grand National, horse show, or race to save her baby brother from the wolves.

Jump for Joy is the early autobiography of a real-life hero, Pat Smythe. This book and others by Smythe, which are still in my library, have been read and reread so many times that the pages are worn and tattered. When in grade school, I memorized the names of the Olympic riders pictured in her book. Smythe was awarded the OBE, the Order of the British Empire, for representing Great Britain with such style and diplomacy as a member of the British Show Jumping Team from 1947 to 1963. Smythe and Brigitte Schockaert, who represented Belgium, were the first two women to ride in Olympic Show Jumping in 1956.

Pat Smythe, OBE, author, and also one of the first women to ride in the Olympics, won at White City in 1951 on Prince Hal, her favorite horse. Photo: Jean Bridel, L'Année Hippique; courtesy of Monica and Lucy Koechlin.

Women were well represented in the Olympic Dressage competition in 1952, the first year this event was opened to women. Lis Hartel won the individual silver medal for Denmark, and was the first woman to claim such an honor in an equestrian sport.

No women and very few civilians had ridden in the Olympics before 1952. Most of the riders were members of their nation's cavalry, and the three-day event was a test of endurance and obedience limited to members of the military.

When American Lana du Pont was permitted to ride in the 1964 Olympics in the three-day, I remember thinking that was "neat" but not pondering the implications of the rule change. I had already ridden at the B level in Pony Club Rallies. The competition followed the three-day format, and how much harder could the Olympics be? I learned the answer to that question in 1968 when I saw my first international level three-day. At the Mexico Olympics, I realized how brave three-day riders are and what challenges they

Liselott Linsenhoff (aboard Piaffe) was the first woman to win dressage gold medals— the team gold in 1968, the individual gold in 1972. Photo: Lichibidsielle BMiLuF; courtesy of Liselott Linsenhoff.

must face on the cross country. I was moved by the courage of the three women representing Ireland, and by the skill of Jane Bullen (now Holderness-Roddam), who was a member of the gold medal–winning British team.

The first woman I saw riding in a steeplechase was Barbara Kraeling (now McWade). She was not the first woman to ride in a steeplechase in the United States, but she was the first winner. She later became a successful trainer, and I watched her saddle the winner of the International Gold Cup when it was held at Rolling Rock, Pennsylvania.

It was at Rolling Rock that I first saw Betty Bird, a woman with an eye for a horse and a very good trainer, gallop Fort Devon. The beauty and grace of Mrs. Bird and Fort Devon riding in the early morning mist of the Western Pennsylvania mountains remain etched in my memory to this day.

Mrs. Bird rode at her peak before rules were changed that would have permitted her to ride in open steeplechases, though she and her sister Sarah Bosley Secor dominated the ladies' races of their day.

Not much controversy surrounded the changing of the rules to include women in dressage and jumping at the Olympics, but major objections were raised before the three-day rules were amended. The three-day was "too dangerous." Objections to permitting women to ride in races at the flat tracks and in steeplechases followed the same lines. Men argued that women were too weak to "hold a horse up."

Women have always understood they can't overpower 1,200 pounds of heart, muscle, and determination, and have used empathy and patience to get the job done. Men aren't strong enough to out-muscle a horse either but are sometimes slower to come to this realization, for men have not been so conditioned to find success through cooperation.

Men are no doubt stronger than women. Their sheer size and mass put men ahead, even in endurance sports such as long-distance running. Some believe this is because the fittest woman is always going to have a slightly higher body fat content than the fittest man. With horses, though, women have been able to compete on an equal basis with men.

Sled dogs have given women the power they need to compete successfully against men, also. The Iditarod, one of the toughest endurance events in the world, covers 1,000-plus miles. Competitors spend an average of eleven days on the trail, bedded down at night in the frozen wastes of winter-time Alaska next to their dog teams. Susan Butcher won the race four times and finished second once. Women compete and finish in the top ten each year.

Women generally need a tool in order to triumph over men in athletic competition. If not a horse or a husky, then a sailboat or a gun. Sailing is the only other Olympic venue in which women may compete against men. The first woman to receive a medal in yachting—in fact, in any Olympic event open to both men and women equally—was Frances Clytie Rivett-Carnac of Great Britain, who paired with her husband to win a gold medal in the 7-meter class in 1908. Women have since competed in yachting events in the Olympics a number of times, but not with the regularity or success of the equestriennes. An all-woman team did score several unprecedented victories in preliminary rounds of the 1995 America's Cup, a sailing competition that featured large, technical, and very expensive 12-meter sailboats.

In riflery, women competed against men in the Olympics for the first time in 1968. Margaret Murdock equalled the score of her American teammate in 1976 in small-bore rifles but, because of a count-back rule regarding tie-breakers, was presented the silver rather than the gold medal. Since then, women have been given their own Olympic shooting events.

In riding, the trend has gone the other way. Some steeplechase meets have eliminated the ladies' race, since women may now enter open competition. Ladies' races remain on the docket at some point-to-points so women can ride without carrying extra lead. The weight for ladies' races is 145 pounds, for open races, 165 and up. In show jumping, separate championships are no longer held for men and women on the international level.

Horse shows at one time offered separate classes for men and for women, recognizing that a woman in a sidesaddle may not be a match for a man riding astride. Women and girls now dominate and are predominate at horse shows, but they did not take over until after 1950. In the 1930s, boys and girls were listed as winners of horsemanship awards in equal numbers. Men rode

Point-to-points still card ladies' races, so small women like Jane Thorne Sloan don't have to carry 50 pounds of lead. Olympic three-day riders have been required to carry 165 pounds since 1950, but in 1996 the FEI appeared poised to lessen this to 156, the same impost women carried before 1950. Photo: Jackie Burke.

by far the most winners in open competition, however, until the middle of the century. The change came, some have speculated, during and after World War II. Women stayed home and ran the stables during the war. After the war, many of those men who before 1940 had filled their days with fox hunts, point-to-points, and polo had to get full-time jobs, leaving the riding to women and the male professionals who remained in the game.

Back in the early part of the century, before women switched to riding astride, some women did reach a high level of achievement in a sidesaddle. Some still do, though one never sees women riding in sidesaddles at races or upper-level jumping competitions.

Before a woman could ride as an equal with a man, she first had to get out of the sidesaddle, and that is where our tale shall begin.

2

Once Upon
a Sidesaddle

IN THE PAST, HORSES WERE USED FOR DOMESTIC ACTIVITIES and for war. Few women went to war, so little was written about women and horses. One can catch a glimpse of women and horses in art, however. Histories of the European courts are also studded with stories of queens on horseback. The nobility filled in the time between wars with hunts. Queens hunted alongside kings, and members of the court—men and women alike—joined in the chase.

Before the fourteenth century, women rode astride, as did men, or they rode pillion—sitting sideways on a cushion behind the rider's saddle. This was an effective method of moving someone from place to place who had no skills in horsemanship.

Horses were the standard form of transportation. You rode or you walked, or traveled in a crude vehicle pulled by horses or oxen. The word *travel* is a variation of the word *travail*, meaning very hard work, which is what getting from one place to the other was before the days of good roads.

The women who rode astride wore split skirts, or in the case of Joan of Arc, armor. If a make-do split skirt was not the proper costume for her

One catches a glimpse of women and horses in the artworks of the day. "The Morning Ride," 19th-century watercolor by Myles Birket Foster. Photo: The Paul Mellon Collection, Virginia Museum of Fine Arts.

destination, a woman was in something of a pickle. If she were all dressed up for a banquet or state occasion, hopping onto the haunches of a horse behind a man was about her only choice.

Perhaps it was this practicality that led Anne of Bohemia (1366-1394), wife of England's Richard II (1367-1400), to introduce the sidesaddle to England. Whatever the source of her inspiration, the queen started a fashion that continued into the twentieth century. Sources do not specify if Anne designed the first sidesaddle or was simply the first historic figure to use one.

If such a saddle had already been invented, Anne most likely would have known about it. Anne's sisters married into the royal courts of Hungary, Austria, and France, so she heard of the latest luxuries and developments in learning then prevalent in the late Middle Ages.

The style of sidesaddle Anne used was like a pack saddle with a horn in front. The woman gripped the horn with one hand and sat sideways, with her feet supported by a wooden platform, or planchette. Essentially, the rider was sitting in a chair without a back. The only pace possible in this insecure position was undoubtedly slow—but there was room for the rider's skirt, which could contain yards of fabric.

Headdresses in Anne's day were "high like horns," and dresses were "long trayned gowns." Court dress became even more elaborate as centuries passed, and one can imagine a lady-in-waiting piled onto a gentle mount with heaps of brocade and petticoats mounding up in front of her. Even the horses' trappings were decorated with plumes and silk and beads.

Women managed this odd manner of riding with varying degrees of success. While staring sideways at the world from those earliest sidesaddles, some of these noblewomen were probably already thinking that there must be a better way. Then, as now, women who had the skill to face squarely forward—said to be a difficult feat even in today's much-improved sidesaddle—had the best time of it.

A forward-thinking Queen Isabella of Spain (1451-1504) must have also been forward looking when she crossed and recrossed war-torn Spain. Through her heroic rides to stare problems directly in the face, Isabella brought a state of stability to her poverty-stricken nation. This wasn't an easy task.

Just months after her coronation in December 1474, Portugal sensed an opportunity and declared war on Spain. At that time, Isabella could muster only 500 horses for her army. She rode from province to province recruiting an army and quelling any dissatisfaction among noblemen and peasants alike. William Prescott, a much respected authority on her reign, described Isabella's journey to rally the troops as a long and painful one made on horseback "with surprising celerity," or speed. He fails to mention—or perhaps expects the delicate reader of the nineteenth century to know—that she was pregnant as she hastened across the broken and difficult ground of Spain in her awkward saddle. We learn this detail from Peggy Liss, a modern biographer, who explains that in May and in the midst of this activity, Isabella gave birth to a stillborn son. By July, Isabella mustered a force of 4,000 men at arms, 8,000 light horses, and 30,000 foot soldiers.

Because she liked horses, or perhaps because she had been caught short, Isabella established a state stud in Andalusia. For breeding stock she drew heavily on the fast, hot-blooded horses of the Moors (Arabs living in Spain). She was well aware of the value of a light cavalry, and the Spanish horses she raised were valued throughout Europe. They were bartered for with gold dust, ivory, and slaves. At the turn of the sixteenth century, one horse was worth twelve slaves.

Isabella favored white or cream-colored horses, and these became known as Isobels. She rode beautifully, and always in a sidesaddle. A gilded saddle with trappings of gold and silver was strapped onto her white horse for state occasions.

Isabella was also a skilled huntress. Her hounds chased hares and deer, bear and boar, and she killed wolves with her own lance.

The first and only great change made to the sidesaddle from Anne of Bohemia's time until the nineteenth century was the addition of a second horn, the invention of Catherine de' Medici (1519-1589). This second horn permitted women to face forward and gain some sense of security by hooking their right leg over the new horn, while still using the original horn as a handhold.

Catherine de' Medici invented the style of sidesaddle that had two horns, used until the 1830s. "A Lady's Hack," oil on canvas by James Ward, 1796. Photo: The Paul Mellon Collection, Upperville, Virginia.

Writers do not speculate about why Anne of Bohemia put women on a sidesaddle in the first place, but guesses have been made about Catherine's motive. One of her ladies-in-waiting suggested the change was made because Catherine had attractive ankles she wished to "display to advantage" riding in her new-style saddle.

If this be true, she certainly had other reasons as well. For one, Catherine, described as small and thin, was determined to hunt, though she was far from being the best rider in the French court. She badly needed to curry favor with her father-in-law Francis I (1494-1547), "whose ardor for the arts was only exceeded by his love of hunting."

The French court, the grandest of the royal courts of that time, was horrified when their crown prince was matched up with the daughter of a merchant. Even the wealth of the Medicis didn't buy Catherine any friends at court, because the Pope, who had arranged the marriage, siphoned off a lion's portion of the dowry. Her ploy with the king worked, and he offered his homely daughter-in-law protection from wagging tongues too ready to criticize her lack of style.

Others suggest that she wanted to be in the hunting field in hopes of winning her husband Henri's heart from her rival, Diane de Poitiers (1499-1566), a legendary hunter and the best rider in the realm. Henri loved sports and hunting and was awed by de Poitiers' knowledge of hounds and her excellent kennels and stables.

De Poitiers, almost twenty years Henri's senior, befriended him at a time when his attractive older brother seemed certain to inherit the throne. When his older brother died unexpectedly, the notorious de Poitiers tightened her hold on Henri to her great financial and social advantage. De Poitiers commanded Henri's attentions from the time he was a boy until his death, but his wife came to win his respect. Catherine was a trusted political confidante and the mother of his ten children.

So small, homely Catherine, described as an intelligent and stubborn woman and one willing to tackle any challenge with boundless energy, learned to hunt and learned to like it.

Catherine continued hunting until she was sixty, in spite of numerous falls, once breaking her leg, another time fracturing her skull, and still another time crashing through a low shed, sustaining a bad and heavy fall that marked her nose "like a sheep of Berri."

Not all women bought the idea of riding sidesaddle, though the longer the sidesaddle was around and the more it was used by royals, the more society believed it was the fit and proper way for a woman to ride.

Public opinion was of no particular consequence to Catherine II of Russia, known as Catherine the Great (1729-1796), so she rode astride and demanded that all women in her court follow suit.

Women in Louis XV's court in France were expected to take riding lessons astride in the manège of Versailles if they wished to hunt. These women rode in long split skirts, high boots, and a tricorn hat.

Marie Antoinette (1755-1793) did not bother with the skirt, but rode in boots and breeches though her attire included an elaborate plumed hat and gold lace jabot. After she became queen, she rode only in a sidesaddle.

Catherine de' Medici's style of sidesaddle continued to be used, with few changes, until the nineteenth century when a third horn was added. Some credit its invention to the French riding master Atelier Pellier, others to the even more famous François Baucher. In his *Dictionnaire Raissone'e d'Equitation,* Baucher wrote that the new saddle gave women "security at all movements of the horse, no matter how brusque or violent."

This third horn is referred to as a leaping head, and once it was added, a-leaping the ladies went. Hunts until the turn of the nineteenth century were something of a glorified royal procession, but with the English Enclosure Acts came fearsome walls, hedges, timber fences, and ditches. Riders had to jump in order to hunt. This was possible with the leaping head. Another improvement about that time was the addition of a balance strap, which kept the saddle more secure and made the horse more comfortable.

In her authoritative book on sidesaddle, *The Saddle of Queens,* Lida Fleitmann Bloodgood likened the invention of the leaping head to the woman's Magna Carta or Declaration of Independence. With the added security the leaping head afforded, women were as secure in the saddle as men, free to fly over the ditches and harrowing thorn hedges, banks and timber fences that sprang up in nineteenth-century England.

In the redesigned sidesaddles, women rested their right leg over the second horn—the one added by Catherine de' Medici. The left leg was supported by a stirrup. When necessary, the woman could push her legs against the horn and the leaping head, thus anchoring herself firmly into the saddle.

Having gotten women into the sidesaddle and put them in a position of security, we will now consider conditions that have shaken most women loose from this fairly comfortable perch.

Several factors came to bear. Women, it is said, fell from sidesaddles less often than they fall from cross saddles, but all agree a fall from a sidesaddle is likely to have serious consequences.

Two of the worst-case scenarios were when a horse reared and fell over backwards and when he fell onto his left side. A woman had little opportunity to get free in either case. Women also could sustain falls from the sidesaddle when a horse quickly changed direction. To avoid this situation, the woman's groom or "pilot"—a woman riding sidesaddle was always accompanied by a man—would take a jump first and go straight after landing, assuring that the woman's horse did not duck suddenly upon landing.

As the twentieth century approached, more and more people were riding and hunting for recreation. Hunting was no longer the sole province of nobility. Riding sidesaddle is a very expensive proposition, and the cost was a mark against it as those with limited incomes took up the sport.

By the turn of the century, a few women were riding astride. By the 1930s, it was about half and half. Women who were riding sidesaddle in the 1930s never switched to cross saddles, and some of these women lived long enough to still be hunting in the 1960s. Even now, a few women continue to hunt sidesaddle in England and Ireland.

Sandra Hoyer, master of the Commonwealth Fox Hounds since 1995 and formerly a whipper-in for the de la Brooke W Foxhounds, has hunted sidesaddle since the 1960s. Hoyer, who is troubled by arthritis in her hip, is much more comfortable during the long hours she spends in the hunt field riding sidesaddle. She contends a woman can do almost anything sidesaddle she can do astride.

With a few exceptions, not many women took up the tradition of riding sidesaddle after the 1930s. A few horse shows continued to offer sidesaddle classes as an interesting diversion, but that was it until the International Sidesaddle Organization was formed in the 1970s. Now more shows offer sidesaddle divisions with three or more classes leading up to a championship, and the American Horse Shows Association awards a national championship.

Back when sidesaddle riding was the norm, Elizabeth "Sis" Worrall's mother, Mrs. Elizabeth Merrill Furness, showed sidesaddle in open competition. Mrs. Furness jumped honest four-foot and four-foot–six-inch timbers—and in a ring, where maneuverability as well as jumping prowess were necessary. Like Mrs. Worrall's grandmother, Mrs. Furness hunted sidesaddle and continued this practice until she was almost seventy and a heart condition ended her days in the field. Mrs. Furness won the first 50-mile division of the Virginia Trail Ride at Hot Springs when she was in her sixties.

The Hot Springs ride is challenging, not just for the distances covered, but also for the testing, mountainous terrain. Mrs. Fletcher Harper, another sidesaddle rider, won the 100-mile division at Hot Springs, as well as the equally mountainous Vermont 100-mile ride, this when she was in her seventies. Mrs. Harper was still competing in 100-mile rides when she was in her eighties. The distance didn't appear excessive to Mrs. Harper, who for a lark had once ridden from her home in Virginia to her place in Geneseo, New York, a distance of about 1,200 miles. Mrs. Harper first sat in a sidesaddle when she was five years old and never rode in any other type of saddle. To correct curvature of the spine, a doctor advised her to switch from a normal sidesaddle, which faces the woman's legs to the near or left side of the horse, to a specially built off-sidesaddle, which turns the legs to the right.

It has been said that women who rode sidesaddle could continue to ride and hunt to an older age than those who rode astride because less strength was needed to hold the rider aboard in a secure position.

Mrs. Fletcher Harper won 100-mile rides in her special off-side sidesaddle.
Photo: Courtesy of Jennifer Youngman.

Mrs. Worrall, who has hunted astride for many years, suspects this is true. "Sis" learned to ride by simply piling on a pony bareback and riding around the stable while her mother and her mother's friends were having their weekly rides. Mrs. Worrall and her sister both grew up riding astride. In spite of family tradition, neither was encouraged to ride sidesaddle, though they both can.

"Maybe mother just saw the end of that style of riding coming, when we were starting to ride," Mrs. Worrall mused, while looking through old albums of the elegant ladies who once graced the hunt fields. Her mother was a visionary in other ways, too. As the founder of Piedmont Vineyard, Mrs. Furness was the first in Virginia to successfully raise the finicky vinifera grape, so prized in making premium wines.

Mrs. Neville Lemmon Atkinson of Spring Hill Farm gave up riding at 87 when her favorite mount had become too old. Photo: The Fauquier Times-Democrat.

Mrs. Worrall said she could not imagine anyone being able to hunt and ride sidesaddle as her mother and the women before her had, because of the expense. To begin with, the horse had to be well schooled. A sidesaddle horse must be big and strong, able to carry the heavy, slightly unwieldy sidesaddle. The perfect horse has a shuffley gait, not the springy forward trot we see in sports horses today, and a flat jump. A horse that arches its back over the top of the big hunt fences would bring a whole new meaning to the term whiplash.

The equipment is very expensive. The saddle must be custom-fitted to each horse and restuffed on a regular basis, because sidesaddles are more prone to cause sore backs in horses than cross saddles do.

PIEDMONT VINEYARDS

HUNT COUNTRY

Mrs. Elizabeth Furness was the first in Virginia to successfully grow vinifera grapes. Her likeness graces the wine labels of the vineyard she established.

Each woman hunting sidesaddle had to have a groom with her. The groom, back in the 1930s and certainly through the centuries before, hacked the horse to the meet for the lady, or at the very least lunged out any good-natured bucks before the woman mounted. A groom was required to get the woman into the saddle. Old books on the subject suggest that two grooms are best, one at the horse's head, and one to hoist his mistress into the saddle, "preserving her modesty lest her skirt become displaced." When not performing these critical duties, he was schooling the horse to the nth degree.

Until well into the nineteenth century, a woman did not wear breeches under her skirt—who, after all, would fit such a garment? Surely not a man. To make do and preserve modesty, women were hampered by miles of skirts and petticoats. This getup must have been most uncomfortable, not to mention dangerous, since the long, trailing skirts were forever getting tangled in hedges and branches. Grooms in those days rode with blankets tied around

Women riding sidesaddle always were accompanied by a groom. Mrs. Marie Sears and Cavanaugh. Photo: Courtesy of Mrs. Elizabeth Worrall.

their waists so their ladies' mounts would become accustomed to dragging yards of billowing cloth. Mrs. Worrall remembered that grooms in her mother's day, and horse sellers for sure, rode sidesaddle to train horses for women.

Women in the 1930s (and those who participate in today's sidesaddle classes at horse shows) were no longer encumbered by long, heavy skirts. They wore breeches covered by aprons. Aprons are abbreviated skirts, longer on the left side than on the right. When mounted, the apron lays flat and neat over the knees, giving it the appearance of a skirt. These have to be tailored to the rider and skillfully cut so they hang just right.

Mrs. Catherine Harts is a contemporary of Mrs. Worrall, but unlike Mrs. Worrall, who has always ridden astride, Mrs. Harts has only ridden sidesaddle. This is not because her father, William P. Hulbert, was a stickler for women riding that way, but because of an incident that occurred when she was seventeen years old.

Her father, known affectionately by residents of Middleburg, Virginia as "Pappy," was one of the most famous horsemen of his day. He played polo, drove a four-in-hand, and hunted with Catherine's mother six days a week. Horses were used to work the farm, and a passel of ponies were kept around for the children to ride. One year, as the date of the Middleburg Horse Show approached, Mr. Hulbert looked in the barn and saw four beautiful, matched chestnuts. Well, the thing to do, her father thought, was to enter the family class. The women in the family—her mother, Catherine, and a sister, then twelve, would ride sidesaddle.

Catherine was big enough to wear a borrowed sidesaddle habit, and her sister, smaller and younger, was somehow pinned into one. Following a tradition begun in the late 1800s (and still in vogue), Catherine, her sister, and mother wore veils with their riding habits. All dressed up and prancing around on a sidesaddle, Catherine felt pretty much like the queen of the castle.

Catherine Hulbert Harts loved the glamour and security of sidesaddle from the time she and her family rode in the Middleburg Horse Show family class. Left to right: Elizabeth and Catherine, Mr. and Mrs. Hulbert. Photo: Courtesy of Catherine Hulbert Harts.

Like other children of the time, Catherine spent her early years riding bareback, and not even in proper riding clothes, but in dresses and bloomers. "Yuck," she comments, as she remembers that indignity.

The Middleburg show was not the fancy "A" show it is today, but a fun show held at Glenwood Park one week before the hunt season began. Having enjoyed this moment of fame at the show, Catherine begged her parents to let her go to the opening meet sidesaddle.

They acquiesced, and shortly after the hounds moved off, an accident occurred. Catherine, in her grandeur, had been trailing along at the back as children were expected to do, when suddenly an adult was yelling to "Go on, go on," trying to clear the accident scene. That forced Catherine to be swept over a jump—her first riding sidesaddle.

"It was the easiest thing I ever did," Mrs. Harts says. "I jumped everything we came to the rest of the day and have never ridden any other way since."

Mr. Hulbert inadvertently started Mrs. Mildred Skinner riding. Mrs. Skinner, at age ninety-nine, could still recite chapter and verse of that fateful day many years earlier.

"I was living in New York at the time but had lots of friends in Virginia and often came down for weekends," Mrs. Skinner remembers.

On one of these occasions, she stayed with the Hulberts, and—no surprise—Mr. Hulbert announced that they would all go riding the next day.

"Impossible," said Mrs. Skinner. The only riding she had ever done was as a child, and this was on very mean ponies that ran her into trees.

Mr. Hulbert said not to worry, he would put her in a sidesaddle. The next morning, he brought around Ruth, one-eyed and not pretty but the prize of the barn because she had a knack for doing everything just right, and for anyone.

So the entourage rode down the driveway to a small jump, which Mr. Hulbert said they were going to jump. "No, I've really never ridden," Mrs. Skinner reminded her host with growing conviction.

Mr. Hulbert sent Catherine and her siblings scrambling over the small jump on their ponies. "There now, if those little children can do it, I'm certain you can," Mr. Hulbert said.

"Well, I did it," Mrs. Skinner said, "and it was the most exciting thing I've ever done." They proceeded to jump every obstacle they came to in that beautiful corner of Orange County Hunt territory. The next day, Mrs. Skinner went fox hunting, and that was it.

Many more weekend trips to Virginia followed, and her marriage to famous and handsome steeplechase rider and horse trainer Jack Skinner led

Mrs. Mildred Skinner loved riding sidesaddle and hunting on Last Thought. Photo: Courtesy of Mildred Skinner.

In a sidesaddle, women could not achieve the forward position needed for Olympic-sized jumps. Kathy Kusner and her Olympic mount Untouchable. Photo: Courtesy of Kathy Kusner.

to many more hunts. Mrs. Skinner was given a horse by the late Stephen Clark, another legendary horseman. The horse had been the sidesaddle mount of his late sister, and Mr. Clark decided Mrs. Skinner should have it. "His name was Last Thought and he was the most perfect horse," Mrs. Skinner recalls. She continued to hunt as long as Last Thought continued to go, then she retired from hunting and riding.

Mrs. Skinner, like Mrs. Harts, contends that riding sidesaddle is easy and a woman can be very secure hunting and jumping in that style of saddle.

In 1912, Belle Beach wrote in her book *Riding and Driving for Women* that the whole idea of women riding astride was an outrage. All well and good for young girls to ride astride to get started, but women's thighs were too round and too weak to grip riding that way, and the idea of a grown woman's figure in breeches was totally preposterous.

Lady Apsley, a top sidesaddle rider in the 1930s and author of *Bridleways Through History*, gave a more balanced account of the advantages and disadvantages of women riding astride compared with riding sidesaddle. She, too, felt a woman was most secure riding sidesaddle and backed this up by counting the number of falls she witnessed in the hunt field taken by women riding astride compared with those taken by women riding sidesaddle. Though almost every fall was from a cross saddle, she admitted women were already learning to ride astride better than those first mavericks had at the turn of the century. Women were better trained to ride astride and were finding saddles that fit better, too. Lady Apsley proposed that women looked most elegant sidesaddle, and they do, judging by entries in horse shows today. She said they were a "perfect credit to their men-folk."

One factor beside the expense that may have spelled the death-knell of sidesaddle as a dominant form of riding was the forward seat, developed at the turn of the century by the Italian cavalry officer Federico Caprilli. In the hunting prints of the nineteenth century, we see that both men and women display the same upright posture. It is impossible to get really forward in a sidesaddle. Some, like Mrs. Furness, and Lady Apsley, who even rode in point-to-points sidesaddle, did better than others, but a true forward seat, needed for an Olympic-sized course, could not be achieved sidesaddle.

A WALL PAINTING NOW IN THE NATIONAL ARCHAEOLOGICAL MUSEUM in Athens, Greece, shows two women in a chariot. The women appear as pleased and happy as any two stylized Greek figures, shown in profile, can look, given that artists in ancient Greece did not portray emotions. Art historians date the fresco at thirteen centuries before Christ and describe the scene as "Noble Ladies of Mycenaean Greece Going Out on a Hunt."

Scientists are not able to prove if prehistoric woman left the cave to help her man hunt mastodons, but we may assume women were hunting from the very beginning. Although the lion is the king of beasts, the lioness is the hunter of the family. It is not surprising that ancient deities of hunting were cast in the female image. Artemis, Greek goddess of the hunt, was born of a wolf. The divine huntress to whom the bounty of the hunt was sacred, this goddess loved the woods and the wild chase, and was in charge of all animals. The Roman equivalent, Diana, ruled over the hunt and also the moon; the Celtic equivalent was the goddess Epona.

Stories of women in the hunt field were recounted in ancient China and Egypt and in other civilizations in which ease of living had risen above subsistence level. Greek philosophers discoursed on the benefit to body and soul of chasing wild game through the fields, an opinion passed down through the ages. What's more, as anyone who has been on a great chase knows, nothing is quite as exhilarating as a gallop on a good horse over testing countryside. For women, hunting offered an opportunity to develop courage and riding skills of the sort now used in today's three-day events.

The hunt field has also been a training ground for philosophers and rulers. Queen Isabella of Spain and Catherine de' Medici (an Italian who was queen consort and regent of France) were hunters and Renaissance women, and so was another French regent, Princess Anne (1460-1522).

Anne, known as Anne of Beaujeu, was interested in the education of women and in hunting. She set up a school in which noblewomen were taught to read, write, and speak Italian, Spanish, and Latin, in addition to their native French. She also gave rise to the Royal White Hounds of France through her stewardship of Soulliard, a staghound that had been given to her father, Louis XI. Soulliard came into her care after a nobleman advised her

Women were determined and brave hunters until forced from the field during the Victorian Age. "The Joys of the Chase, or the Rising Woman and the Falling Man," oil on canvas by John Collet, exhibited 1780. Photo: The Paul Mellon Collection, Upperville, Virginia.

father to entrust the care of the magnificent hound to the wisest lady in his realm. Louis XI, known as the Spider King for his disagreeable personality and habits, replied that there were no wise women, but that his daughter Anne was less foolish than most.

Soulliard and his offspring hunted only deer, as fox hunter George Washington learned to his disappointment when he received "large hounds of great presence" as a gift from the Marquis de Lafayette following the Revolutionary War.

In the Middle Ages it was understood that there were three categories of game: those that ran from you, such as the hart (stag) and hare; those that ran at you, such as the bear and boar; and those that depended on their wits, such as the fox.

The fox, once considered a varmint, was at first hunted for the purpose of eradication. Those engaged in this low form of activity were derisively called rat catchers. (Informal hunting attire is still referred to as "rat catcher.") However, after the wolf had been hunted to extinction in England by the eighteenth century and large tracts of forest needed for game such as bear were cut down, the fox started looking pretty good. Hunters came to view the wily fox as a quick and clever quarry.

The first woman master of foxhounds was the first Marchioness of Salisbury, who took up her hunting horn and whip for the Hatfield Hunt from her husband in 1775. Meriel Buxton offered information about Lady Salisbury in *Ladies of the Chase*. Her hounds were described as dwarf foxhounds, steady, with fine noses. The field consisted of forty to eighty followers, including gentlemen, farmers and horse dealers. Lady Salisbury retired in 1812 at age seventy.

During Lady Salisbury's day, hounds were slow, and the pace was ponderous across the heavy ground of England, as yet undrained by ditches. Hunts lasted twelve to fourteen hours. The only obstacles encountered were brooks, banks, or the occasional park wall, and these were leaped from a standstill, or riders dismounted and led horses over.

By the nineteenth century, the sport was changing, and not in a way that led more women to follow in Lady Salisbury's bootsteps.

Hunting was no longer a game of sheer physical stamina. Women, in the sidesaddle of Catherine de' Medici's design, were not in a position to ride at the scorching pace that was made possible by the draining of the countryside for farming. Jumps were getting bigger and much more frequent due to a number of enclosure acts passed during the reign of George III (1760-1820). Farmers built stout fences, dug ditches, and planted hedgerows to contain their stock.

English fox hunting became the province of gentlemen intent on riding at a steeplechasing speed. After a day of sport, the foxhunters caroused into the night at dinners, toasting one and all. To placate the ladies, left almost entirely on the sidelines, hunts began hosting traditional festive hunt balls.

Women were never barred from the hunt field in France, where stags were hunted through large forests crisscrossed by allées. "The Field Check in a Wood," oil on canvas by Alfred de Dreux (1810-1860). Photo: The Paul Mellon Collection, Virginia Museum of Fine Arts.

In France, attitude and opportunity allowed women to continue riding to hounds even after their English sisters had been vanquished. Then, as now, the French chased stags through vast forests along *allées,* or trails, with little jumping necessary.

Women in France were still well educated and considered "charming companions during the hours of reason." Not so in England, where Samuel Johnson wrote that a man wanted a wife who could cook a good meal, not one who could read Greek. It became the habit of many an Englishwoman to hide her knowledge and intelligence.

This attitude toward women represented a gradual but steady decline in status. At the time of the Norman Invasion (1066), women enjoyed the right to own property and most of the same rights as men. This right and others were lost by Victorian times, to the extent that widows were not automatically granted custody of their own children. John Stuart Mill (1806-1873) wrote in *The Subjection of Women* that the condition of women was hard to turn around, because it was based on instinct, feelings, and custom, not on reason and fact.

Queen Elizabeth I of England (1533-1603) loved to hunt and was very learned. She read, wrote, and/or spoke Greek, Latin, Hebrew, French, Spanish, Italian, and Welsh. Women rulers who followed were less well educated. Elizabeth's successor, James I (1566-1625), disapproved of the education of women. His great-granddaughter, Queen Mary II (1662-1694), who co-ruled with her husband, William of Orange, was taught only French. Her main interest was the domestic arts, which made her a wonderful housekeeper, but a dull conversationalist. Queen Anne (1665-1714), who ascended the throne in 1702, loved hunting and racing but was said to be woefully lacking in education. She did not possess even rudimentary skills in geography and history, subjects ruling monarchs really should understand. In eighteenth-century England, women's academies emphasized sewing, dancing, domestic arts, menu planning, and singing. Because women were not taught academic subjects, they were considered less intelligent than men.

By the 1830s, a woman's place was in the home. The sidesaddle had been improved, and women might have taken to the field again, but society was against the idea. Those women who actually did hunt were considered fast for all the wrong reasons. Only wives and daughters of masters of foxhounds (MFH) could get away with hunting, and they often held hereditary titles, which offered them a double protection from criticism.

R.L. Surtees (1803-1864) included very few female foxhunters in his humorous books about country life. Lucy Glitters, "of late of the stage but tolerably virtuous," hunts with Sir Harry Scattercash's hounds in *Mr. Sponge's Hunting Tour* (1850). She marries Mr. Sponge in the closing pages of that book, but has been abandoned by her cad of a husband when she reappears in *Mr. Romford's Hounds* (1860). In this book, Lucy suits up in her impeccable hunting garb to help Mr. Romford sell horses. Lucy was patterned after well-known figures in nineteenth-century England who earned notoriety and large dealer's fees by hustling sales horses in the hunt field and in Hyde Park.

Miss de Glancey in *Ask Mama* (1858) represents the other type of female reported to frequent the hunting field back then—those quite helpless women, who were a hindrance to the sport, and who hunted only for a husband. Surtees has little use for her sort and ends Miss de Glancey's hunt in a driving thunderstorm that drenches her hair and habit.

Anthony Trollope includes a chapter on "The Lady Who Rides to Hounds" in *Hunting Sketches*, first published in 1865. Trollope wrote that when three or four ladies joined the field, the men straightened up and behaved with more decorum. He discounts stories of flirtation in the hunt

Queen Victoria wearing the long and cumbersome skirt traditionally worn by women riders of the day. "Queen Victoria on Horseback," bronze by Thomas Thornycroft, 1854. Photo: The Paul Mellon Collection, Upperville, Virginia.

field, suggesting that the parlor or dance floor made a much better arena for courting. Trollope did not like a woman who demanded special favors, but noted the majority of women in the field loved hunting and rode as true a line as a man, jumping whatever fierce obstacles they encountered.

Trollope wrote during the reign of Queen Victoria (1837-1901), when the Queen in particular and all women in general were held in worshipful respect. Men felt they must protect helpless women, and this attitude could be tedious for both sexes in the hunting field. Men feared a good day's hunting would be lost due to an inept female. On the flip side, however, women got lots of unsolicited assistance. In her recollections of hunting as a girl in the 1880s, Mrs. Julian Keith of Warrenton, Virginia wrote that men were always leaping off their horses to lower barways for her that she "could have cleared on a cart horse."

In England, one hundred years of prejudice against women in the hunting field was finally overcome by the triumphant hunting tour of Empress Elizabeth of Austria (1837-1898).

Elizabeth, consort of Prince Franz Joseph of Austria, had already established a fox hunt in Hungary at Godollo when she set her heart on hunting in England. After viewing a hunt there, she realized sport at Godollo was but a pale imitation, with fences low and far between and foxes that dug into sandy soil after a brief run.

To prepare for her English trip, Elizabeth, in her sidesaddle, practiced riding over the steeplechase course in Vienna, the only way she could approximate the speed of English hunting and the all-out pace at which they took jumps.

Elizabeth made a good show her first hunting day in England but was disappointed that the speed had been cut by deep footing. She immediately set out to charm Lord Spencer, the master of the Pytchley, and to finagle an invitation to hunt. Elizabeth, a world-class charmer, was invited by Lord Spencer to a private hunt in her honor the very next day. Even with such short notice, a gallery of three hundred came to watch the beautiful Empress. Bay Middleton, the boldest rider of his time, was appointed her "pilot." (As mentioned earlier, a woman riding sidesaddle was always guided by a man when hunting, since she could not mount by herself, due to the voluminous skirts of riding habits.) Middleton did not relish the prospect of being impeded by some foreign empress riding on his coattails, but the Empress proved she could keep up with Middleton, and each goaded the other to take bigger jumps and more chances. As stories of their performances spread, even more admirers lined the roads to the hunts, and riders in the field swelled to five hundred.

During her days in England, Elizabeth proved women were capable of following the hounds with speed and courage, and in the grandest style. She broke the ice for women who wished to hunt, and from that time forward, they were welcome in the English hunting field.

Women in Ireland did not actually need a leg-up, for they could hunt if they were able. Though Elizabeth was not such a novelty there, the Irish admired her courage and skill. Her fans lined the roads when she traveled to the hunts, throwing flowers and presenting her with bouquets.

In the seventeenth century, settlers to America from the British Isles brought with them hounds, horses, and a love of hunting. Foxhounds were first brought to America in 1650 by Robert Brooke, an English immigrant to Maryland. Hunting in the English fashion flourished under Thomas, the 6th Baron of Fairfax (1693-1781), in pre-Revolutionary days.

Lord Fairfax's land, a vast tract of prime territory that encompassed all the best of the current Virginia Hunt Country, was surveyed by young George Washington. Through his association with Fairfax, our founding father developed a lifelong love of fox hunting and patterned his style after that of the English nobleman.

Washington's diaries are a rich source of information about his hunting. These were carefully preserved because he was, after all, a very famous man. To learn about women who hunted in America is a much trickier business because not much has been written on the subject. Women do show up in early photographs of fox hunts, and by the turn of the twentieth century, women—though much in the minority—are seen riding both astride and sidesaddle.

J. Blan Van Urk, the great hunting scribe of the 1930s, included what information he could glean about women in the hunting field in *The Story of American Foxhunting*. He supposed that proportionately more women hunted in 1800 than did in 1900 and that in 1939 there were as many women in the hunt field as there were men. Exactly what brought Van Urk to this conclusion is not told, but his sources include books printed in the eighteenth and nineteenth centuries, sporting journals of the nineteenth century, and a wealth of private letters and diaries.

Van Urk found a newspaper advertisement from 1760 for "Ladies' Hunting Side Saddles." He wrote that the editor of *Porter's Spirit of the Times* in 1856 instituted a ladies' column to generate interest in foxhunting among women. A doctor writing about the same time in the *College Journal of Cincinnati* suggested that an interest in riding and foxhunting could cure women of sick headaches, nervousness, palpitations, and so on.

By the 1930s, women, some riding astride and some sidesaddle, hunted in equal numbers to men. Mrs. T. A. Randolph and Mrs. Elizabeth Merrill Furness. Photo: Courtesy of Mrs. Elizabeth Worrall.

Van Urk let a story tell itself when possible, and included in his history a lengthy, fascinating letter written by Mrs. Gertrude Rives Potts, the first woman in America recognized as a master of foxhounds by the Masters of Foxhounds Association (MFHA). She wrote that her ancestor, Dr. Thomas Walker, imported the foundation stock of her pack, the Castle Hill Hounds, from England in 1742. Walker served on the staff of General George Washington.

Mrs. Potts recounted the history of her family, the hunt, and her mastership. Before petitioning the MFHA, she visited landowners and persuaded seventy-two of them to give her permission to ride across their land.

Mrs. Viola Winmill (1884–1913) was elected joint master of the Warrenton Hunt in 1925. She hunted six days a week and was a well-known carriage whip. Her large carriage collection was donated to the Carriage Museum at Morven Park, Leesburg, Virginia. Photo: Robert McClanahan.

Mrs. Potts would ride out before daylight, in hopes of finding a mountain fox down hunting in the grassland of Albemarle County, Virginia. Such a visiting fox was often chased all the way back to the craggy peaks of the Blue Ridge Mountains, and on such occasions, Mrs. Potts would not ride home until late at night.

Many women have followed Mrs. Potts as masters of their respective hunts. A review of MFHA yearbooks lists no women masters in 1923, ten in 1928, fifteen in 1931, and twenty-one in 1935. Fourteen women served as master during the war years. During World War II, a few hunts handed over the mastership to women for the duration of the war, some hunts continued as usual, and some hunts became inactive. There were twenty-eight women masters by 1945, but only twenty-seven ten years later. By 1955, forty-two of the ninety-two hunts had listed a woman master at some time in their history. Since then, the numbers have risen steadily. In 1995, 120 women were listed as master or joint master of the 170 hunts then recognized by the MHFA. Some women were listed as Miss, some as Mrs.; some served alone, some as joint masters with their husbands, some with other women, and some with other men.

Nancy Penn-Smith Hannum (Mrs. John B.) came to her position as head of Mr. Stewart's Cheshire Foxhounds as a joint master with her stepfather, W. Plunket Stewart. In 1995, Mrs. Hannum celebrated fifty years of mastership with this austere pack, highly regarded for the quality of its hounds and excellence of its hunt country.

Mrs. Hannum is not certain how old she was when she started hunting, although she has a photograph of herself at age four, hunting with her mother and father. She said, "I wasn't on a lead rein, so I must have hunted some before that."

That photo was taken in Virginia. Mrs. Hannum's maternal grandfather, E.H. Harriman, brought the Orange County Hunt from Orange County, New York, to its present-day home in The Plains, Virginia. Her great-grandfather hunted in the best grass country of England. Her own father, R. Penn Smith Jr., was master of Orange County, and after he died suddenly when she was ten, her mother took over the mastership for a brief time before moving the family to Unionville, Pennsylvania.

Mrs. Hannum said of the move, "I thought I was going to the hinterlands. I hunted with American hounds, and up in Pennsylvania they hunted with English hounds. It seemed like an unspeakable comedown. I just couldn't imagine such a thing."

Young Nancy had been tutored on the superiority of American hounds while sitting on a hillside with her father and his huntsman. Well, she supposed in the rest of her life she would never be as smart as she was at age ten, but Mrs. Hannum has certainly learned a lot about English hounds from her stepfather, the founder of the Cheshire Foxhounds. Mr. Stewart believed the English hounds' lack of cry and hunting drive so criticized by the Virginians could be improved through selective breeding. She was taught about hound breeding and many other things as the daughter of a master.

When asked about her impressions of women in the hunting field when she was young, Mrs. Hannum said she took no more notice of them there than she would have in the audience at the theater.

"Fox hunting is a non-competitive sport. Women have always been welcome to participate," she said.

Women in her mother's day hunted sidesaddle. At age four, Nancy and her friends learned to ride astride under the tutelage of Captain Gaylord, an Englishman who taught riding lessons on Long Island in the 1920s. Mrs. Hannum has always ridden astride, though she learned to ride sidesaddle, and sometimes rode sidesaddle to school horses for her mother.

Mrs. Hannum was only three years out of college when she became joint master in 1945. She said it was the most natural thing on earth for her. "I was born to do it," Mrs. Hannum said simply. Since earliest childhood she had watched her father, her mother, and her stepfather cope with the intricacies of land-owner relationships and hound breeding.

With more modesty than necessary for a woman of her achievements, Mrs. Hannum said, "I've really only been basking in reflected glory all these years, as caretaker of a pack and country well-started by others."

Mrs. Hannum's stewardship of the land continues through the Cheshire Hunt Conservancy, which she founded for the purpose of preserving the rural nature of the country she has loved, and over which she has hunted the English hounds she has come to admire.

Another famous woman master was Mrs. Theodora Ayer Randolph, who headed the Piedmont Fox Hounds from 1954 until her death in 1996. Piedmont, founded in 1840 and the oldest hunt in America, rates with the Cheshire as one of America's very best. Piedmont even won the right to that title when it triumphed in a famous hunting competition held in 1905. (Renowned hunting folk from around the country attended the match, including Mrs. Potts and Mrs. Hannum's grandfather.

Mrs. Theodora Randolph, née Ayer, grew up near the Myopia Hunt Club in Boston, and as her daughter, Nina Bonnie, said, "Mummy caught the horse disease early."

Mrs. Randolph began her lifelong love of hunting during her school days in Virginia, where she found comfort after the death of her mother. She

Mrs. Nancy Hannum, who celebrated her fiftieth year as Master of Mr. Stewart's Cheshire Hounds in 1995, was not long out of college when this photograph was taken for Sports Illustrated *in 1952. Photo: Toni Frissell; courtesy of The Library of Congress.*

graduated in 1924 from Foxcroft, the famous preparatory school of so many fine riders and outstanding women in other fields. The school was founded in 1914 by the famous Miss Charlotte Noland. The head mistress, in immaculate sidesaddle attire, always hosted Middleburg Hunt's Thanksgiving meet on the school lawn and served as that hunt's master from 1932 to 1946. In case there was any doubt about her interest, Foxcroft's intramural teams are named the Foxes and the Hounds.

After Theo Ayer's marriage to Robert Winthrop, she moved to Long Island, but always kept a little place in Virginia so she could come down to hunt. After divorcing Winthrop (father of Nina, Amory, and Theodora), she lived in Virginia full time and married Dr. A.C. Randolph, master of Piedmont. When Dr. Randolph's health failed, she became master. "I did not particularly want to be master," Mrs. Randolph said, "but someone has to lead and to do the job."

Nina Bonnie, in an address given when Mrs. Randolph received the Jimmy Williams Lifetime Achievement Award from the American Horse Shows Association (AHSA), said, "Mummy wasn't a committee member or a joiner. She led by example and was absolutely committed to quality in everything she did."

Albert Poe, who came on as huntsman in 1954 when Mrs. Randolph and her neighbor Paul Mellon became joint masters, said hunting in his view, and many others would agree, hit its height when Mrs. Randolph was master.

Mrs. Randolph led the field, and there has never been a better field master, Poe said. "The hounds came first, and the huntsman second. She kept the riders an entire field behind the hounds. A whipper-in would ride back and forth to keep her informed of what was going on.

"The first five minutes of a run are critical. The hounds need to settle in on their fox, without having to fight their way through a bunch of riders to get to the huntsman," Poe continued. "With Mrs. Randolph's help, I could get twenty couple on the scent, and they would run as one pack. You don't see that today. No one these days understands hunting the way Mrs. Randolph did."

Once the pack settled in, the followers were in for quite a ride.

Today, the hunt has installed chicken coop jumps, lower than the line fences and with a slant to make jumping easier, but Poe said that in 1954, the country wasn't paneled the way it is today. They jumped the big post and rails at Mr. Mellon's and faced stone walls topped with two heavy riders (poles) at the old Phipps place (now Rockburn).

"Those jumps were five feet high. The first time I faced one of those big walls, I stopped to try to let down one of the riders, but it was wired up. Mrs. [Bettina] Ward, wife of the master of the Middleburg Hunt, was riding up front with Mrs. Randolph. She shouted to me to 'jump or get out of the way.' Those women were game!"

Poe said that Mrs. Randolph kept twenty-one hunters fit and ready to go. She took first pick, and Poe got second pick. Mrs. Randolph always owned breeding stallions and raised her own homebreds. Black Gang, one of her best-known stallions, was from the War Admiral line. If his progeny could race, they did race, otherwise they were shown or hunted, according to her daughter. Bonnie, a top competitor in the amateur owner division, said, "Mummy had a great eye for a horse."

The women in Albert Poe's day were a hard-riding lot. Mrs. Elizabeth Furness, noted judge and conformation expert Sallie Sexton, and Mrs. T. A. Randolph ride through Upperville (ca. 1940). Photo: Courtesy of Gary Baker.

Mrs. Randolph bred and raced Bon Nouvel, twice Eclipse Award winner and a Hall of Fame steeplechase horse. She bred many good show hunters, including War Dress, three times champion of the National Horse Show, and Army Wife, AHSA champion hunter.

She could also spot a good rider. It was Mrs. Randolph who helped Kathy Kusner along by providing her with a horse for the Olympic team tryouts. The horse was High Noon, "very mean, but one that could jump," Mrs. Randolph remembered.

Besides the hounds and field, the master is also responsible for the countryside, and Mrs. Randolph had her own special method of undertaking this task, Poe remembered.

"She had a real farm, 1,700 acres, and raised all sorts of stock and crops," Poe related. "When we were hunting and saw a thin horse, Mrs. Randolph would send around a truckload of hay. Once we noticed crops hadn't been harvested because the farmer had broken both arms, so Mrs. Randolph sent

Mrs. Theo Randolph offers young Kathy Kusner advice at a Virginia point-to-point.
Photo: Courtesy of Gary Baker.

her farmhands over to pick corn. She would never take money for things like this, and no one realizes how many acts of kindness like that she committed through the years."

Hunting was the most popular rural sport through much of the past millennium. It was natural for women to participate, and they did, except for a brief period during the Victorian Age in England. It was natural, too, that they moved into positions of leadership. The first women masters came to their posts through family ties. Their competent performance opened the way for the many others who have followed.

For women to gain a toehold in the racing world, the next arena of challenge, they had to rely on an overwhelming love of horses and a good measure of raw courage.

4

Pioneers on the Backstretch

By the 1930s, women in America hunted both astride and sidesaddle. They rode in horse shows, almost always in ladies' or amateur classes, and were still a long way from riding in the Olympics. They rode in ladies' races at the local point-to-points (informal steeplechases sponsored by hunt clubs), usually astride, but sometimes sidesaddle, and were still a long way from being sanctioned as race riders. Even so, women were beginning to make inroads at the race track.

Racing in the 1930s was a national pastime, rivaled only by baseball as a spectator sport. The "backside" of the track (stable side) was a man's world. Women who did venture into the Sport of Kings often did so at considerable personal sacrifice.

Life was tough for those early pioneers. Judy Johnson, the second woman to be awarded a trainer's license in New York, was very successful both with flat horses and steeplechasers, yet she experienced many valleys between the peaks of her life.

She once told *The Maryland Horse,* "Life is like a wheel. The bottom turns to be the top just as it turns to be the bottom. If you don't get too big a head while you are at the top, you won't hurt too badly when things go the other way."

This rare sketch of women riding in a horse race dates back to the 19th century. "A Ladies' Horse Race," pen and ink, Thomas Henry Nicholson, 1839. Photo: The Paul Mellon Collection, Virginia Museum of Fine Arts.

In the interview, which appeared in September 1968's *The Maryland Horse,* Johnson observed that 1952 had been a particularly tough year. In the space of 40 days, her mother and one of her brothers died, and her entire stable of horses perished in a fire at Belmont Park. She counted 1961 as testing as well, when her long-time backer Thomas T. Mott (of applesauce fame) died, and she was once again without a horse. She fought back after these tragedies. Her last test must have been particularly hard, for she suffered a stroke and was paralyzed in 1971, and spent her last seven years in a nursing home. Johnson, quoted in the same 1968 article, said, "You can lose your job . . . everything, and come back. But if you lose your nerve, you've had it. As long as you've got two eyes, two legs—and your nerve—nothing is impossible."

Johnson, like some of the other pioneers in the sport, left no husband, children, or grandchildren behind to mourn or remember. The details of their lives come to us from magazine and newspaper articles, and through the memories of those who met these very special women along the way.

Peter Winants, who served as editor, then publisher of *The Chronicle of the Horse,* and before that on the staff of *The Maryland Horse,* said "Judy Johnson was the first woman to hold a jockey's license. I'm sure of it. She rode back in the '40s."

Marge Dance, whose father founded *The Maryland Horse*, not only remembered Miss Johnson, but knew exactly where to find the right issues of the magazine.

Clips from *The Maryland Horse* and the newspapers of the day that were saved by Joe Richards III, son of one of her prominent owners, make clear what a hard, lonely life Johnson must have lived.

Richards confirmed that life for women who chose the turf as a career wasn't easy. Even so, Johnson made a great success of her profession. "She was a wonderful horsewoman, well respected around the race track," Richards said.

His first memories of Johnson date back to when he was age eight and had just started hunting. "I remember her hat," Richards volunteered. Johnson always wore a soft wool "roller" hat; it was her trademark and set square on her head in every photograph one can find.

Richards' father was the secretary of the Redland Hunt. Redland's master was Thomas Mott, Johnson's most important owner. She trained many top 'chasers for Mott. During the 1940s and 1950s, Mott's stable won every major steeplechase at one time or another and some years had the leading money earner.

Johnson hunted with Redland, and Richards remembered that she was always around, so it was natural that his father, Joe Richards Jr., selected her to train his good flat horses. His best horse, and hers too, according to her own accounts, was Sir Beau, owned under the partnership of Tri-Colour Stable. Johnson purchased Sir Beau as a yearling at the Eastern Fall Sale for the reasonable sum of $4,500. He went on to win stakes as a two- and three-year old and to start in the Preakness—the first horse trained by a woman to do so—and the Belmont Stakes.

Johnson was the only one of horse trainer Edward Johnson's eleven children to take up the trade. Her father, American by birth, worked at Chantilly, France's major training center, then at its English equivalent, Newmarket. When her father brought Papyrus, an English Derby winner, to Belmont for a match race in 1923, the family moved back to America.

Help was hard to find, so 15-year-old Judy galloped horses for her father. She attracted a lot of attention, being the only "lass" among the stable lads and exercise boys. Not everyone welcomed a girl on the backside, but soon enough she was an accepted and, as Richards remembered, well-respected part of the scene.

Judy Johnson's best horse was Sir Beau, shown here after winning the Marlboro Nursery at Marlboro, Maryland, in 1967. Johnson, second from the left, sports her traditional soft wool hat. Joe Richards III, the son of the owner of Tri-Colour Stable, is on the right. Photo: Courtesy of Joe Richards III.

When, in 1936, Mary Hirsch, the daughter of the famous trainer Max Hirsch, was awarded a trainer's license, Johnson's supporters encouraged her to try for her license, too. Within a week, Johnson was granted her license and was in the training business.

Steeplechase horses were always her specialty, so during World War II, when women were driving trucks and riveting rivets, Johnson applied for her steeplechase rider's license in Maryland and was promptly granted one. She raced in Maryland for the first time on April 27, 1943. She rode more often in Canada than in Maryland and won seven races, all on the other side of the border. When the war ended, she left race riding to the men and went back to doing what she liked best—training horses.

Howard "Gelo" Hall, clerk and patrol judge for the Maryland Racing Commission, remembered that Miss Judy was respected by one and all. If many backsiders at that time were unconvinced that women belonged there, she earned their respect, and none had a disparaging remark about Johnson.

"She was a credit to the business," Hall said. "She provided the criteria for women coming later. She was well liked and well received—and she won races. She made a lot of jockeys—including Willie Graham, a black rider. She gave a lot of boys a chance who wouldn't have gotten to ride otherwise."

On the other side of the Atlantic, Nancy Sweet-Escott was beginning her career. She was born in 1907, the daughter of a clergyman.

Although her family had no particular interest in horses, she was, like many young girls, a self-professed "horse nut." Back then, horsemen and horse dealers were plentiful, and it wasn't long until enterprising Nancy was schooling and helping to sell ponies. Early on, she became recognized as particularly skillful with a rogue.

Perhaps her affinity for difficult horses drew her into a most unsuitable marriage. Her family never forgave her when, at age nineteen, she married a just-divorced forty-two-year-old alcoholic. When sober, her husband was a magnificent horseman, and with him she engaged in many horse enterprises. The couple trained race horses and steeplechasers. As her husband's drinking problem didn't lead to much stability, the couple was always branching out into other projects to keep a roof over their heads. During World War II, Sweet-Escott ran a twenty-two-room hotel she furnished for pennies and for which she made the bread, butter, cheese, and sausage. All the while, she hunted, rode exercise on the race horses, and tended to any equine injuries.

When her husband's alcoholism brought him under, Sweet-Escott trained their race horses unofficially, as women in England could not hold a training license until 1966. (Mrs. Florence Nagle and Norah Wilmot were the first. Mrs. Nagle brought suit against the Jockey Club, and the High Court ruled that it must abandon its policy of denying women training licenses based on their sex. Until that time, Mrs. Nagle and Ms. Wilmot trained by obtaining licenses in the name of their head stable lads. Ms. Wilmot had trained in this fashion for thirty-six years before she was allowed to start a runner in her own name. Not content to rest on her laurels after defeating the Jockey Club, the eighty-two-year-old Mrs. Nagle, who bred Irish Wolfhounds, fought sex discrimination in the Kennel Club.)

When Sweet-Escott's husband became more than she could handle, she accepted an invitation to visit America and arrived with a six-month visa in January 1953. Sweet-Escott, age forty-five, stayed in America and began a career with horses.

Through her biography, *The Clergyman's Daughter,* Sweet-Escott spelled out just what it was like for a woman, with no resources other than her talent, to come to a new country and try to make it as a horse trainer.

For the next fifteen years, she lived the life of a gypsy, traveling from track to track, sometimes with a stableful of good horses, more often with a cripple or two and a job washing dishes. She often slept in a back room of the diners where she worked to make ends meet. Her career was based on rogues and cripples. People sent her horses as a course of last resort—if no one else could do anything with an animal, Sweet-Escott got a try. She treated horses with bowed tendons with such success that she became known as a witch doctor.

At age sixty, Sweet-Escott was tired of the traveling. She set up a little training center in Southern Pines, North Carolina, her favorite port of call. Owners like Taylor Hardin, a horseman of the old school and very strict about the way he wanted things done, always sent his yearlings down to be broken by Sweet-Escott. From Hardin's select band of brood mares came one stakes-winning filly after another, broken by Sweet-Escott.

After ten happy years at her training center, Sweet-Escott was struck down by arthritis. In 1983 at age seventy-six, she moved in with her good friend Virginia "Ginnie" Moss, who invited Sweet-Escott to spend the rest of her life as Mrs. Moss's guest.

Like Johnson, there are no children or family to remember Sweet-Escott today. Those who remember meeting her speak of what a fine lady she was. Her book suggests no matter how hard her life was, she never lost her sense of humor or sense of fun.

Fred Kohler, Virginia bloodstock agent, remembered "Nancy Sweet" as very colorful, with an enthusiastic and joyful countenance. She was tall and willowy, and the first on the dance floor at any party. Kohler said she could really "swing a leg." Into old age, tall Nancy could out-Charleston or out-jitterbug anybody, and easily kick her leg over the head of her partner.

Training horses is not an easy or glamorous life, but it can be a satisfying one, according to Barbara Kees, who has been training race horses in Maryland since 1948. As hard as some of the years were, both her daughter and son have stayed in the horse business.

Kees was the horse-crazy child of non-horsey parents. She grew up during the Depression, and a horse was a luxury the family just couldn't afford. Eventually her mother managed to buy her a pony and build a barn. Horse shows and later marriage followed. Her former husband was also crazy about horses, so the couple moved to Maryland because back then "every house had a horse trailer, and everyone had a horse in their yard." The couple bought a farm, where Mrs. Kees still lives and trains.

Almost fifty years after her first training venture, she still rubs, mucks, and hot walks. These days, she leaves the galloping to her daughter, Sherry Rudolph. Her son, Tim Kees, trains show horses. The family keeps about thirty to thirty-five horses on their farm.

Among Kees' best horses were South Bend, winner of twenty-eight races, and Row Boat, winner of twenty-five. She's raised two children and managed to put them both through college. She said, unlike many people, she loves her job. "Training horses gets you up in the morning," Kees said, "and makes you look forward to the rest of the day."

Sally Roszel, one of the best point-to-point riders of her day, served as MFH of the Orange County Hunt. She is pictured in Orange County hunt country in front of her ancestral home. Photo: Courtesy of Jennifer Youngman.

Sally Roszel, one of the best women point-to-point riders from the mid-40s until about 1960, was not a trainer but a rider. She wanted to get her jockey's license, and some of the most respected steeplechase trainers, like Jack Skinner, came to her aid, but for naught. Judy Johnson had been a wartime phenomenon, and Maryland stewards weren't in the mood to grant another woman a license.

Like Sweet-Escott, many horses that came Roszel's way were tough ones. "They'd put me on the bad horses before the men would get on them," Roszel remembered.

Many of the horses she raced were too tough to hunt. Any of the rogues that were hunted went out in a severe long-shanked pelham, but had only a mild snaffle in their mouth when brought to the paddock for Roszel to ride.

"Sometimes I didn't get on the horses before the race, which was all right because some of them were so bad. One time when I did gallop a horse I was due to race, his regular rider, a big, strong black man, said quietly afterwards that the horse usually ran away with him," Roszel remembered.

She had ridden a horse (this one was a nice one) for the late Jean Bowman, and Bowman recommended her to Emmett Roberts, a leading steeplechase rider who was based in Middleburg. He had forty-plus horses in training, and Roszel was hired to help him gallop and school. The horses were trained to jump either timber or steeplechase fences, which were big and stiff, unlike the standardized plastic fences used at all the race meets today.

When Roberts moved his string to Pimlico, Roszel went up to gallop and school there. At that time, Pimlico held a jump race every day as part of its race card and kept schooling fences in the infield. Traditionally, a big schooling session was held on Maryland Hunt Cup day, attended by many in the area for the races. Roszel remembered with delight that the late Rigan McKinney, America's winningest amateur steeplechase jockey and a member of the Horse Racing Hall of Fame, watched her jump head-and-head with two other riders, then told Roberts he "wanted to buy the boy's contract," referring to Sally.

Her fame grew to the point that she caught the track officials' attention. They decided a woman should not be schooling horses over fences, even though ten years before, a woman had ridden in steeplechases there. The decision was made that Roszel could continue galloping horses, but it was "too dangerous" for her to school.

Eventually, the same thing happened in Middleburg. Back in the 1950s, local horsemen used the steeplechase schooling grounds at Stephen Clark's on the Halfway Road near Hill School. Roszel schooled up to five horses a day there. In addition to the horses she galloped and schooled, she would break yearlings, getting on up to fourteen a day.

"I was very strong back then," Roszel remembered. "A horse could go right down on its nose, and I didn't come off."

Even so, Mr. Clark decided a woman shouldn't be schooling horses—too dangerous. Roszel figured it was a macho thing—the male riders didn't like losing the business to a woman.

"I don't want to sound bitter," Roszel said, "but I was disappointed. I really loved schooling a horse over a big fence."

A woman Roszel followed around the course in many a ladies' race, Betty Bosley Bird, also lost opportunities because she was a female. Bird's mother and father were both race horse trainers. "My sister and I won a lot of ladies' races because we rode the best horses," Bird said.

"When my horse Count Stefan was entered in the 1946 Maryland Hunt Cup, my father asked the committee if I could ride," Bird said. "The reply was 'no.' I remember being very disappointed."

Her brother was given the ride on her horse. The horse made a bad mistake at fence six but stayed on his feet to finish second.

Accounts of the race describe Count Stefan as, "as tractable and personable a horse as ever ran in the Hunt Cup." A few weeks after the Hunt Cup, the six-year-old grey won the ladies' hunter championship at Devon with his owner aboard. Other than his appearance in the Hunt Cup, Count Stefan was always ridden by his owner. She hunted him and also taught him tricks—to buck, bite or kick on command.

By 1953, Betty Bird, at that time still a Bosley, had her own training barn. She trained some point-to-point horses for their owners to ride, and others for owners who simply wanted their horses to run. She did much of the schooling and rode her charges when possible in flat races or ladies' point-to-points so she could judge their fitness first-hand. This was particularly true of Marchized, whom she described as an unsound horse, but one with extraordinary jumping ability and movement. Betty did not own him, and his owner, Cynthia Cannon, received a tempting offer for him before the 1953 Maryland Hunt Cup. Betty pleaded, "Don't sell him, Cynthia. Please let me find a buyer so he can stay in my barn. He's a horse that can win the Hunt Cup."

Marchized was described in the race's history as young and inexperienced, with just two starts on the flat and three in ladies' point-to-points, all of which he won with Betty in the saddle. John Rossell wrote in *History of the Maryland Hunt Cup*, "Miss Elizabeth Bosley had trained the horse with the loving care and attention characteristic of her and there seemed no question as he paraded in the paddock that he was ready for the test at hand."

With the famous D.M. "Mikey" Smithwick in the irons, Marchized won the race. Betty said, "I just loved Marchized as a horse. He was a wonderful animal."

Her other Maryland Hunt Cup winner was not so lovable. In fact, he was ornery. Fort Devon was also owned by Cynthia Cannon, and she really didn't know what to do with him. She bought him as a three-year-old at the Dublin Horse Show. He proved big and mean. First one trainer, then another tried him and gave up. Betty flew to Ireland to ride him in the sidesaddle classes at Dublin, but when she arrived at his stable, the trainer didn't want to let her ride him. "He'll hurt you," she was warned.

"This is silly," she said, insisting that having traveled so far, she should at least try the horse. "He started to rear—and as a horse with perfect balance, he could just stand there on his hind feet swaying back and forth—but I kicked him and hit him. He moved off, and I started patting him—getting his mind off himself. He moved like a pony but every now and then would hit his stride, and I could tell he was a lovely mover."

Betty, who was now married, talked her husband into shipping the horse back to Pennsylvania. It would be nice to say Fort Devon became a lamb. He may have looked like a lamb, but during his years with Bird, he managed to lay his teeth into every one of her girl grooms.

Fort Devon did prove a perfect hunter—her very favorite. He had a light mouth and wonderful way of going. He loved to hunt, so Bird hunted the otherwise contrary horse into racing fitness. Fort Devon ran his very best races right after the hunt season. Fort Devon won the Hunt Cup in 1976, and within a year or two had added victories in the Grand National Point-to-Point, Pennsylvania Hunt Cup, and any other race Bird chose to try.

"He had done everything we could ask here, so we sent him to England," Bird said.

There, he won his first time out, racing over the big, stiff English steeplechase fences. Bird said, "I can't remember what else he won, but he was always a great favorite with the British racing public. One time he bit a press photographer who kept inching up to us in the paddock. I warned the man to back off, but he didn't listen. Fort Devon never laid his ears back—he just grabbed the man. The press just loved things like that."

Betty's mother, Elizabeth Cromwell Bosley, also had a way with difficult horses. Sarah Bosley Secor, Betty's sister, said her mother loved a challenge. The famous trainer Max Hirsch discovered this trait and sent her his problems. Mrs. Secor remembers one occasion on which her mother felt she had bitten off more than she could chew.

Betty Bird and Fort Devon melded into as fluid a pair as ever graced the hunting field or exercise track. Photo: Courtesy of Betty Bird.

"Mr. Hirsch had the richest owners and was always importing the best horses from England and Europe. One horse that he brought over killed his handler on the boat and killed another groom when he got to New York. The horse was sent to Mother. When he got off the train in Maryland and she saw what a mean eye he had, she wanted to send him straight back.

"Fate intervened, and the horse got badly hurt while running around in his paddock. He was too weak to fight, and Mother nursed him back to health. The horse trusted Mother completely and would do anything for her."

Not surprisingly, Hirsch kept their barn full. He also sent his daughter Mary down to spend the summer with the Bosley family. Mrs. Secor said that Mary was a sweet girl who loved horses. Mrs. Bosley taught Mary to ride. In 1936, Mary Hirsch was the first woman to be granted a training license in the state of New York.

Though Mrs. Bosley helped with Hirsch's horses and had an occasional steeplechaser, she did not get her training license for the flat track until Chase Me came along in 1933.

Chase Me, like many of the Bosley's horses, was bred to race but used instead as a riding horse, as was most often the case. Chase Me was Sarah's mount, and following the family tradition, she made a pet out of him and taught him tricks. One day her mother wanted to breeze a well-bred but lazy horse Max Hirsch had sent to them, and Sarah galloped Chase Me along beside to give the other horse incentive to run. Sarah's horse trounced her mother's promising steeplechaser, and as a result, Chase Me was promptly put in training. Before his first race, Chase Me, remembering one of his tricks, tried to shake hands with the starter at Havre de Grace (a Maryland track no longer in existence), then easily won the race. He won many more races, and for a time Hollywood considered making a movie about him. Having been taught to steal handkerchiefs, he would always remove his bandages and hand them to his groom.

After Chase Me, Mrs. Bosley took to training flat horses. Mrs. Secor said, "Early in her marriage, Mother was given three good brood mares with racing bloodlines. She just made their offspring, who were bred to race, into hunters, because she wasn't interested in racing then. After Chase Me, she said she was sorry she hadn't gotten into the racing earlier."

Mrs. Bosley got her training license in Maryland in 1933. Later, she spent a good deal of time racing horses in New York. Like other big owners and trainers of the day, she stayed in a "bungalow" at Belmont.

In 1940, she was killed in an auto accident. She was just forty years old and had sixty-three horses in training. Her owners included Ogden Phipps, A.C. Bostwick, and Elizabeth Arden—the major owners of the day. She was the first woman trainer to nominate a horse for the Kentucky Derby, though it went lame on the eve of the race and was unable to start.

According to all accounts, Beth Bosley could have been licensed to ride either flat horses or steeplechases had she not been a woman. Her daughter Betty Bird raced the horses she herself trained whenever she could. She knew the weaknesses and condition of the horses she trained better than anyone. She did not get an opportunity to race them as a woman today might, nor did Roszel, but a woman's day to ride into the limelight was steadily approaching.

Dressage—A Perfect Sport for Women

RIDING EVENTS WERE PART OF THE ANCIENT OLYMPICS. Chariot races were included as early as 680 B.C., and mounted horse races were added in 648 B.C. After a centuries-long hiatus, the first modern Olympics were staged in 1896. Olympic equestrian competition, which replaced the annual world military riding championships, was added at the Stockholm games in 1912. The three disciplines of riding competition of the modern Olympics are dressage, show jumping, and the three-day event, which was formerly referred to as "the military."

Show jumping and the three-day include elements of thrills, falls, speed, and jumping. Grand prix dressage, on the other hand, has the deliberateness and civility of ballet.

Dressage at the Olympic level is about rhythm and grace, strength and obedience, developed through years of systematic training. As a competitive sport, it compares with figure skating. Required figures are performed in a regulation-sized arena, 20 meters (roughly 66 feet) by 60 meters (about 180 feet). At the Olympics, five judges award scores of 1 to 10 for each of thirty-three movements, plus four additional marks for general impressions.

Swiss rider Christine Stuckelberger and Granat, and a big hug after winning the gold medal in 1976. Photos: Gamecock, from the Morven Park Collection; The Chronicle of the Horse.

Donnan Sharp Plumb Monk represented the United States in the 1968 Olympics. Photo: Douglas Graham; courtesy of The Fauquier Times-Democrat.

Donnan Sharp Monk (formerly Mrs. Plumb), who rode on the United States dressage team in the 1968 Olympics, thinks women are well suited for dressage.

"Women can get in a horse's head and bond with the animal," Monk said. "Women ride with their minds, not their bodies. A woman would never try to overpower a horse to show it what they wanted it to do."

Most men's eyes glaze over at the very thought of spending eight years to produce a grand prix–level dressage horse. In the early 1960s, many of Monk's fellow riders at Gladstone, New Jersey, site of the U.S. Equestrian Team (USET) training grounds, figured those who could ride chose jumping or the three-day, and all others chose dressage.

Gen. George Patton, World War II hero, probably expressed American male sentiment in comments made after watching a special exhibition of the Royal Lipizzaners. The performance was given by the tatters of the Spanish Riding School on ill-fed Lipizzaners that had survived World War II, hidden deep in the hills. As the war ended and the Russians approached, riding school members rode for the lives of the horses, which they wanted to put under the protection of the American army. The soul-stirring scene was re-created in a Walt Disney movie, but after seeing the real thing, Patton wrote in his diary that he couldn't understand why "obviously fit young men would spend their days teaching horses to wriggle their butts." He did save the Lipizzaners because, he wrote, teaching horses to dance made as much sense to him as opera.

Patton's attitude toward the high schooling of horses may reflect a cultural rather than sexual trait, since European dressage masters and teachers are usually men. Germans, Swedes, and Swiss have the discipline, tradition, and training to appreciate the intricacy of dressage. The Spanish Riding School, showcase for the Lipizzaners Patton saved, was established in 1572. Starting in about 1500, the European nobility began to build manèges (indoor riding halls) in which riding evolved into an art form featuring leaps and piaffes, "the high school." In theory, horses were being taught evasive movements for the battlefield; in fact, kings and their courts wiled away hours refining their horsemanship. Depending on the court, century, and circumstances, women were sometimes permitted to take lessons as well.

In spite of their proclivity toward dressage and this long tradition, women were nonetheless barred by the Fédération Equestre International (FEI) from riding in Olympic dressage until 1952.

The FEI was formed in 1921 to perfect the rules of international equestrian competition, including the modern Olympics. Conferences were held under the initiative of France and Sweden to create a set of regulations and guidelines for equestrian competition.

The introduction to the 1929 rule book contends the FEI "has given a new impetus to advanced equitation, which was being forgotten by a modern world enamored of speed. To compare the various schools of instruction was for the horse enthusiast a powerful incentive to better training and this result is manifested by the progress which has been noted at each successive official competition."

The fundamental principles of dressage as defined by the FEI are the basis of all rational equitation. The 1938 rule book states that dressage aims to render the horse "agreeable, at the same time keen yet submissive."

Under the 1938 FEI rules, dressage was open only to military officers and amateurs. A definition for amateurs was given, and while women could qualify as amateurs, Rule 214 stated that Amazons (women riders) could not participate in the equitation events of the Olympic Games. If otherwise qualified, women could participate in all other international competitions recognized by the FEI. In 1950, the FEI rules were revised, and women finally got their chance for Olympic glory in the dressage competition at Helsinki.

Marjorie Haines Gill, the first American woman to ride in the Olympics, did not take up dressage with that goal in mind. She had seen photographs of newly immigrated German dressage master Fritz Stecken performing the piaffe and wanted to know what it was all about. Gill said, "Seeing a horse carry himself like that was magical."

Fritz Stecken trained Marjorie Gill, the first American woman to ride in the Olympics. His mount, Noble, performs the piaffe. Photo: Courtesy of Marjorie Gill.

Gill had ridden all of her life. Horses were always available through a farmer friend and her aunt, Violet Haines, who owned a riding school just next door. She most often rode jumpers because those competitions carried the best money prizes, important since Gill's equestrian endeavors were not backed by monied parents. Gill also rode in one of the first three-day events in Pennsylvania, placing first and second on her aunt's two mares.

With a taste for dressage from the three-day and fascination with Stecken's photos, Gill set out for New York in hopes of taking lessons from the great man himself. Only two people were teaching dressage in the United States at that time, Richard Watjen (who instructed Olympian Karen McIntosh, and later Donnan Sharp) and Stecken. Dressage in the early 1950s was about as foreign as the term itself—the word is French, with no English equivalent. Americans, other than army officers trained for international competition, knew nothing of dressage training. There was some "circus" dressage around, but little of the real thing and no competitions.

Stecken taught at Sleepy Hollow Country Club in New York. Initially, he had few students, though he had almost everyone interested in learning dressage at that time. Among Stecken's early disciples was Mrs. Archie Dean, whose interest turned to dressage from the popular equitation classes of the day after three of her children won prestigious horsemanship medals at Madison Square Garden.

Gill arrived in New York in 1951, age twenty and fresh out of art school. She had $1,500 in her war chest, lived on $5 a week, and ate mostly cereal. She rode a bicycle everywhere since the expense of a car was out of the question. Mrs. Dean befriended Gill, whose small supply of cash ran out within three months. Gill said, "The kind Mrs. Dean gave me two dinners a week in exchange for sewing lessons. The Deans' food, support, and inspiration, along with sewing orders, kept me going."

Gill took lessons on Nobel, the horse she had seen in the photo, and Flying Dutchman, a German gelding with high school dressage training. Flying Dutchman had been brought to this country by the U.S. Army as war booty.

When asked about Flying Dutchman, Jimmy Wofford, son of John W. Wofford, the first president of the United States Equestrian Team (USET), chuckled and said, "Many are aware that Patton saved the Lipizzaners from the Russians, but hardly anyone knows that Patton, a polo player and master of foxhounds, kept an eye out for good horses during the entire war. When the war was over, he gathered up these horses and had the U.S. government ship them home."

The American army liberated 400 horses, of which 247 were Lipizzaners. These horses otherwise would have been taken as war booty by the Russians, who were bent on destroying the horses, which represented to them the last vestiges of imperial rule. Among the non-Lipizzaners were German horses of Olympic caliber, like Flying Dutchman, Rascal, and Bill Biddle. Many of the liberated horses were brought to the army remount at Front Royal, Virginia, and there George Greenhalgh of nearby Clarke County purchased Flying Dutchman. The horse was re-schooled for the three-day and in 1949 won the first Olympic trial for an American civilian three-day team. After this interesting exercise, the Greenhalghs sent the horse to Stecken, who retrained him for grand prix dressage. Wofford, who rode in the 1968 and 1972 Olympics, said, "The Germans were very powerful in the equestrian events at the 1936 Olympics (three team gold medals in three events, three individual gold medals, along with the individual silver in dressage). They would have been awesome had the games been held in 1940."

The Olympics were canceled in 1940 and not held again until 1948. Gen. Dwight D. Eisenhower reactivated a mounted cavalry unit at Ft. Riley in 1946 for the purpose of preparing officers for the Olympics. The few American officers that competed in Europe in 1948 did so by permission of their commanders, and represented not the United States, but Occupation Forces.

German tanks had unofficially rendered horses inviable during World War II, and in 1949, President Harry Truman officially closed the army remount stations across the country, ending the horse cavalry once and for all.

A lone army officer (Lt. Gordon Wright) represented the U.S. in international competition at Madison Square Garden in 1949. It was apparent that if the United States was to be represented in equestrian events in the 1952 Olympics, a civilian team would have to be fielded. Before the 1949 National Horse Show ended, the seed of what was to become the USET was formed. The group, headed by Colonel Wofford, was active by 1950.

Though civilian teams were to represent America in the 1952 Olympics, some of the riders chosen had an army background. Capt. Robert Borg, who represented the U.S. in 1948, led the list for the dressage team, and schooled the three-day horses in dressage, as well. Borg, who also rode in 1956, said in addition to thirty-five remount horses leased from the army, the USET had a number of German horses, at various stages of training, at its disposal.

Flying Dutchman was the most experienced of the available mounts. With the path cleared for women to compete, Stecken selected Gill, though inexperienced, as his pick to prepare for the first U.S. civilian Olympic team. Her progress was watched from the heels of the master by Jessica Newberry Ransehousen, who was to ride in the 1960, 1964, and 1988 Olympics. Stecken fitted Flying Dutchman for the task and promoted Gill to the hilt.

The (male military) establishment was not enamored about having a young woman on the team, but could not deny Gill her chance. Flying Dutchman had been carefully schooled by Stecken, who was the most experienced teacher in the United States at that time. Stecken was from a famous German dressage family and had himself earned the highest score recorded in grand prix competition at Berlin.

So Gill, along with other potential team members, was sent to Germany to gain experience in competing. She caught pneumonia on the boat going over, already in a weakened condition from too little to eat and too much to do.

Gill's story is amazing when considered today. She made the step from successful jumper rider to high school dressage rider in one year. This was possible, Gill said, because of Stecken's instruction and because the horse she rode, Flying Dutchman, knew the correct movements.

The German trip was funded by the USET. The budget for that first international trip was mighty tight, and there was no support system for the riders who went. Newspaper accounts called them the "shoestring team," so scanty was funding.

For financial and political reasons, Stecken could not go to Germany with Gill. So the young woman with less than a year's experience with this new thing called dressage was sent alone to cope the best she could.

Stecken had primed Flying Dutchman for the job, and when Gill got to Germany, she placed in her first three shows. Gill said, "We Americans trying to ride dressage must have been a funny lot to those well-schooled Europeans. Yet I was successful, perhaps riding on Stecken's reputation."

For her international debut, competing in a sport she had only seen performed as a demonstration, Gill was on her own. "I just kept trying to remember what Fritz told me. That's all I could do. I felt that they (other male riders trying for the team) didn't want me there."

A young woman on a captured German horse? Considering the scenario more than forty years hence, Ransehousen speculated that Gill's impressions were correct. "There would have been a lot of people who wouldn't have wanted her there."

The longer Gill was away from her teacher, the more her performance suffered. Finally it was arranged for her to get some help from a former instructor from the Spanish Riding School. That offered a little relief, but even so, Gill said she wasn't ready to face the experienced horses and riders.

Teams traveling with the USET back then received very little technical support. Ransehousen remembered that as late as 1960, the van driver hired to take her to the Olympic dressage event had no idea how to get to the competition and got lost in Rome. The horse finally arrived less than thirty minutes before Ransehousen was due to ride in the Olympics. The men who formed the USET raised funds but didn't engage in strategic planning. Riders back then just had to deal with the conditions they found.

Gill said, "I really don't remember much about riding in the Olympics. I wasn't up to the competition. Dutch was bold and giving, but there was

Marjorie Haines Gill, the first woman to ride for the United States, warms up Flying Dutchman for the 1952 Olympics. Photo: Deutsche Press Agentur; courtesy of Marjorie Gill.

some doubt whether he would be sound enough to compete. The trip on the boat was difficult for all the horses. An Argentine vet saved the day for Dutch, and his treatment was the only reason the horse could compete at all.

"For the Olympics, my parents and friends were there to give me much support. I remember going into the arena thinking I didn't want to go off course. Friends said I looked sad, and I can see that in photos from back then. A lot of things can hurt you, taking away energy, that you don't quite realize at the time."

She finished a respectable seventeenth. Borg was eleventh, and Hartmann Pauly was twenty-seventh. The team was sixth, not a disgrace. The only times army teams did any better were in 1932, when they won the bronze, and in 1948, winning the silver (with then–Lieutenant Borg). This first try by a civilian team was not an embarrassment.

When the team returned to the United States, Gill and Borg made a lasting impression on crowds at Madison Square Garden that fall with a pas de deux (a dressage exhibition performed by two riders). For years afterwards, riders would come up and tell Gill that was their first exposure to dressage, and they began to learn the discipline after seeing that performance.

Then, the single Marjorie Haines married Harry Gill, a talented jumper trainer who owned many champions, including Idle Dice, ridden to fame by Rodney Jenkins. Because jumping was Harry's sport, Marjorie turned her attention back in that direction. In one streak, Marjorie won thirty-three straight jumper championships.

By 1956 the path had been cleared for women to ride in the jumping phase of the Olympics. Gill's consistently good performance in big classes put her in a position to try for the jumping team, but she said the moment had passed. The Gills were parents of their first child, and Marjorie no longer was interested.

Gill has continued to use balance and other techniques learned through dressage in the development of the couple's Thoroughbred jumper prospects. Gill feels that helping a horse to love his work, the quality she had so admired in Stecken, is a rider's highest and greatest achievement. Gill still schools young horses and has produced a video of guidelines for balancing the horse and rider.

Gill was not the only woman to ride in the 1952 Olympics. Lis Hartel, a Dane, not only competed but also won the individual silver medal. Hartel, the first woman to win an individual medal in equestrian competition, repeated this feat by again winning the silver in 1956.

Her wins were all the more amazing because Hartel had been paralyzed by polio in 1944. She was twenty-three at the time, and the mother of a two-year-old.

Lis Hartel and Jubilee, individual silver medalist in 1952 and 1956, gave exhibitions all over Europe (shown here in her native Denmark) and at the National Horse Show in New York. Photo: Courtesy of Lis Hartel.

Mrs. Hartel wrote, "After polio hit me, rather severely, I must say I decided to make a maximum effort to get into the saddle again, notwithstanding the fact that doctors told me I would never be able to ride again.

"I succeeded and restarted riding in dressage competitions winning the Nordic riding games in '51 and in '52. My efforts were crowned with the silver medal in 1952. It was the first time women had competed equally with men in the equestrian games, and this really brought my name into the limelight worldwide, because not only was it a woman, but a handicapped woman! I won the world championships in dressage in 1954, and again a silver medal in the Olympics in 1956."

Polio had attacked the ligaments behind Hartel's knees, weakening and distorting the lower leg. Hartel still did not possess full use of her lower legs in 1952 and could not get on and off a horse without assistance.

How could it be possible in a sport as demanding as dressage for someone lacking lower leg strength to excel?

Hartel wrote, "Riding is not a question of strength only, or then the horse would win over the rider! It is a question of balance and how your seat, back and hips are applied."

Mrs. Margarita Serrell, one of the first Americans to earn credentials as an FEI dressage judge, said, "Hartel proved dressage is not all about leg."

Hartel stayed with Mrs. Serrell when she performed at Madison Square Garden in 1954. Mrs. Serrell said that Hartel was special, her horse Jubilee was special, and her trainer Gunther Andersen was special too. She said, "They were admirable to watch."

Hartel seemed capable of evoking the difficult grand prix movements from Jubilee without moving a muscle. Ransehousen, who had the opportunity to train with Andersen and lived at the time with Hartel, said, "Hartel had very little use of one leg. Even so, Hartel, with the help of her trainer, kept Jubilee going beautifully.

"Hartel is a fine person. The judges liked her a great deal. She was easy to like. Her basics were very good, and she looked wonderful on a horse. Jubilee lacked a great piaffe, but there were many good things about him."

Comments on Hartel's ride published by Baron de Trannoy, president of the FEI, reflect Ransehousen's observations. He criticized Hartel's piaffes but praised much of her work. Under general comments, de Trannoy noted that the rider had a very good seat but often the action of the legs was insufficient.

In those days, the five Olympic judges devoted part of their energy to calculating scores to put their nation's team ahead and other nations behind. This practice was so prevalent that team competition in dressage was dropped in the 1960 Olympics, to be reinstated in 1964 with a proviso that the high and low score be dropped, a safety measure which could later be abandoned.

In 1956, Hartel was a victim of jingoistic judging, and this, perhaps, cost her the individual gold medal. She had placed second behind Henri St. Cyr in 1952. In 1956, only 10 points separated the two, and the Swedish judge placed St. Cyr, his countryman, 26 points above Hartel, though no other judge separated them by more than 3 marks. When the scores were first posted, Hartel was less than 10 points behind St. Cyr, which, according to the rules, required a ride-off. Hartel was ready to ride into the Olympic arena when all of a sudden the president of the jury (Swedish) changed his figures so that St. Cyr was a clear winner of the individual gold and Sweden of the team gold.

Finn Hartel, her husband of fifty-five years, wrote, "It was a dirty trick which was commented on in the press worldwide. The culprit was never allowed to judge again!"

If 1956 was a year of both triumph and disappointment for Hartel, it was mostly a year of disappointment for the American dressage team. In 1952, Gill had achieved respectable performances on a German horse trained by Germany's best masters. Flying Dutchman and other German horses were too old to go to the 1956 Olympics, and the good army horses were fading too. Talent for the U.S. dressage team was at its lowest ebb.

There were still few competitions in the U.S. in which riders could gain experience. Victor Hugo-Vidal, whose former wife Elaine Shirley Watt rode on the 1956 team, said, "A couple of times a year the better riders would come together to be evaluated. Shirley, as a woman, was not made to feel welcome, but she earned a place on the team, so she got to go to the Olympics."

Watt was an orphan, adopted by an older maiden lady who gave her an opportunity to ride. Watt made the best of it, winning the National Horse Show Medal in 1947 and other horsemanship medals for hunter seat, saddle seat, and western riding.

"She got into dressage because she loved to train animals," said Hugo-Vidal, who is himself one of the nation's preeminent hunter trainers. "She trained things I didn't know could be trained, like a skunk."

Watt worked with Stecken but found the German system too inflexible for her Thoroughbred horses, and turned to James Fillis. Fillis's father, also named James Fillis, was an Englishman who trained the Cadre Noir in France, then the Officers' Cavalry School in Russia before World War I. The influence of the senior Fillis could still be seen in the Russian riders who claimed Olympic dressage medals in 1960, 1964, 1968, and 1972. The horses that carried the Russian riders to medals seemed to skim the surface of the dressage arena and to dance through the difficult high school movements. The younger Fillis was himself very old when he helped Watt but agreed to train her for one year.

Watt's experiences at the Olympics, according to her former husband, mirrored those of Gill's. The team establishment ignored her. Unlike Gill, Watt did not even have the benefit of attending any European competition prior to the 1956 Olympics in Stockholm. Her horse, Connecticut Yankee, was ill the day of the competition and was only marginally well enough to go. Watt placed 30th. After his trip to the Olympics, Connecticut Yankee, a Thoroughbred stallion, excelled as a hunter and jumper. Hugo-Vidal said that in today's world Connecticut Yankee would have been very useful as a sport horse sire.

Watt did not try out for another team. After the Olympics, she started dropping things and losing her balance. She would fall without explanation.

She was finally diagnosed as having multiple sclerosis (MS) and died in what seemed to Hugo-Vidal like a very short time.

The United States could not field a dressage team for the 1956 games. Borg, the only other American to ride, placed 17th. If 1956 was a lean year for Americans, it was a triumph for women and offered a taste of things to come. Not only did Hartel win the silver, but a German woman, Liselott Linsenhoff, won the individual bronze medal and led an all-woman German team to the team silver.

Ransehousen also had the privilege of training with and boarding with Linsenhoff. She said, "She was an excellent sportsman. I learned everything I know about competing from her. She always rode to win and wanted to win, but she exhibited grace in defeat.

"She liked a challenge, and at the time we trained together, she rode a very sensitive Thoroughbred who would piaffe at the drop of a hat, making the halt at X [this is how all dressage tests begin and end] especially difficult.

"Liselott was most hospitable. At competitions, she would invite the whole international community back to her room in the evening for drinks and discussion of the day's events."

In fact, Linsenhoff took Ransehousen in to train with her coach, Herbert Kuckluk, after Ransehousen's first international competition. Ransehousen said, "I wanted to remain in Germany, and Liselott was kind enough to invite me to stay."

Linsenhoff was very strict and disciplined. Ransehousen learned that from her, and German as well. "She would speak to me in German at home, repeating and gesturing until I understood."

Linsenhoff received a team gold in 1968 in Mexico. No woman earned an individual medal in dressage from 1956 until 1972, but that year Linsenhoff climbed onto the podium as individual gold medal winner, the first woman so honored. She also claimed the team silver in 1972, bringing her total of Olympic medals to five.

Ransehousen got her first chance to ride in the Olympics in 1960. In 1960 and 1964 her teammate was the brightest star on the American dressage scene, the wealthy, beautiful Patricia Galvin.

Galvin wanted to be an actress, Ransehousen remembered, but that was not an occupation John Galvin would approve for his daughter. It suited him better when Trish expressed an interest in eventing, so he purchased Grasshopper, later used by Michael Page for four straight Pan-American and Olympic teams. Mr. Galvin bought other good horses, eventers and jumpers as well, and invited the three-day squad to train at his ranch in California. When Trish decided she didn't like riding the three-day (women weren't allowed to ride in that event in the Olympics until 1964) and turned to dressage, her father engaged as her instructor Henri St. Cyr (winner of the individual gold in 1952 and 1956 and the only person to manage back-to-back victories in dressage until Nicole Uphoff of West Germany claimed the gold in the 1988 and 1992 Olympics). St. Cyr brought his medal-winning horses as Galvin's school masters, but she didn't like riding them. The horse she liked was an Irish hunter named Rath Patrick.

Rath Patrick had been imported to Canada as a hunter prospect, but he took a disliking to jumping and was schooled for dressage. Rath Patrick and his trainer, Capt. Leonard Lafond, French by birth and a self-taught dressage rider, represented Canada in the 1955 Pan-American Games and in the 1956 Olympics, placing eighteenth.

Liselott Linsenhoff won five Olympic medals, including two golds on her champion Piaffe. Photo: Courtesy of Liselott Linsenhoff.

Lafond and Rath Patrick then immigrated to California. Lafond, re-membered as a kind, nice person, became Galvin's teacher in 1958 and Rath Patrick her school master.

Galvin wrote, "It was an incredible sensation to be on a horse that re-sponded to a fingertip, a minute shift of weight, or the brush of a heel."

They complemented one another, Ransehousen said. Galvin was small and pretty, and Rath Patrick was a large horse that carried her well. He had a good passage and wonderful extensions. Galvin wrote that the horse could change leads every stride at the canter with such ease and perfect tempo, he gave the impression of a child skipping.

Mrs. Serrell said, "Standing still, Rath Patrick was ugly, but when he and Patricia came up the center line to start their tests, they were what dressage was all about."

The very next year, in 1959, Rath Patrick and Galvin earned the gold medal at the Pan-American Games in Chicago. In the 1960 Olympics in Rome, Galvin had the sixth highest score, the best finish by an American civilian in the Olympics up to that time. In 1976, Hilda Gurney had the fourth best score in team competition, anchoring the USET's bronze-medal winning performance, and Dorothy Morkis was fifth in individual competi-tion. Of the military teams, Capt. Hiram Tuttle won the bronze in 1932, and Capt. Isaac Kitts finished sixth the same year, with Lieutenant Borg fourth in 1948.

Even though his daughter had placed so well, Ransehousen said she felt Mr. Galvin was disappointed and did not attend the 1964 Olympics in Tokyo, where Galvin finished eighth, after claiming her second Pan-American gold medal in 1963 at São Paulo in the meantime. With Galvin's strong finish in Tokyo, Ransehousen in fourteenth place, and Karen McIntosh in seven-teenth, the American team finished fourth, not a medal-winning perfor-mance, but the best finish by an American civilian team until 1976. The USET again claimed the bronze in 1992 and 1996.

Ransehousen's background could hardly have been more different from Galvin's. Her parents met her constant expressed interest in horses during childhood by buying her yet another statue of a horse or a lamp with a horse on it. When at age six her parents said they would not buy her a horse, she started scrimping and saving to get one for herself. By age twelve, she had saved up $181, enough to purchase "a gray horse with lovely dark eyes." In retrospect, Ransehousen wrote that Patches was a long-bodied, heavyset, thick-necked little horse, but one with a wonderful disposition.

Once she had a horse, her parents, who had both had unhappy experiences riding as children, decided it was their place to make certain their daughter was safe and well trained.

Ransehousen said horsemanship classes like the Medal and the Maclay were the big thing for young riders in the early 1950s. She herself probably would have gone that route except the late Gordon Wright, dean of the stylish American seat and teacher of the equally influential George Morris, was in ill-health that summer and not taking on new students.

Since Wright wasn't available, Mrs. Archie Dean, a family friend who was taking an interest in dressage, suggested that Ransehousen take lessons from Fritz Stecken, who was newly arrived in this country.

Though a fluke had brought Ransehousen to dressage, she was hooked. Unlike some riders who learned a little dressage, then moved on to other disciplines, Ransehousen has continued in the sport to this day.

Ransehousen said riders like herself, who "did it the hard way," found a lot about Galvin to envy. Still, Ransehousen said with a chuckle, "Patricia took me on one whale of a trip through Spain in a new red Alfa Romeo her father had given her."

A great commotion was always made about Galvin. Mrs. Serrell said, "I wonder what Patricia thought about all the publicity. She was a retiring person, and it must have been hard on her."

After Tokyo, Galvin married a prince and moved to France. She dropped out of the dressage scene.

Ransehousen once again represented the United States in the 1988 Olympics, finishing seventeenth. She has represented America in the Pan-American Games and World Championships. She has won many honors in competition in Europe, including the right to wear the green armband, designating her as leading rider at the Aachen show in Germany, the pinnacle of dressage competition.

Ransehousen continues to ride and school her own horses, teach, and give clinics, and has four times served as Chef d'Equipe of the USET dressage team—at the 1992 and 1996 Olympics and at two World Championships. In this position she has made certain that her teams do not have to hunt for the Olympic stadium on competition day!

Her own daughter, Missy Ransehousen, is one of America's rising event riders. Eventing was not an option when Ransehousen's international career began, nor was it when Donnan Sharp started training with the USET. Like Galvin, Sharp began her career as an event rider in the early 1960s but switched to dressage because women could not ride in the three-day until 1964.

Jessica Newberry Ransehousen rode in the 1960 and 1964 Olympics, raised a family, and came back to ride Orpheus in Seoul, 1988. Photo: John Strassburger, The Chronicle of the Horse.

Dressage was the only option for women back in 1952. The door would soon open a little wider, and by 1956, women were permitted to ride in Olympic jumping. Women have done very well in jumping, as we shall soon see, but in dressage they have been dominant. From 1972 forward, every individual gold medal in the Olympics, with the exception of Reiner Klimke's win in 1984, has been claimed by a woman, and in 1988, all three individual medals were won by women. Women, as Donnan Sharp alleged, are well suited for dressage.

Jumping to the Forefront, or
The Only Flower Strong Enough

PRIOR TO WORLD WAR II, the Olympic equestrian events were effectively limited to cavalry officers on active duty. An increasing number of civilians participated in the 1948 Olympics, but women were still prohibited. Then women were permitted to ride in dressage in 1952, but not in grand prix jumping. Four years later, women finally got their chance to jump in the Olympics, thanks to a rule change in 1953.

> *FEI Rules, 1953, Article 3, paragraph 9. Status of horsewomen—*
> *Horsewomen are subject to the same rules as men . . . Horsewomen are*
> *excluded from the Three Day Event.*

Drawn from FEI rules of the same year is a description of the Olympic Grand Prix Jumping Competition:

> *This event will take place in the Olympic Stadium . . . Each competitor*
> *jumps two separate rounds over the course and, if the necessity arises, there is*
> *a compulsory jump-off to decide the winners of the prizes. There must be 13*
> *or 14 obstacles necessitating 16 to 20 jumps. The height of the jumps may*
> *vary between 1 m. 30 and 1 m. 60 [about 4'3" to 5'3"]. There must be a*
> *water jump with the water at least 4 m. 50 wide [about 14 1/2'] . . . Jumps*

involving a spread [open ditches, oxers, etc.] are from 1 m. 50 to 2 m. 20 [about 4'11" to 7'3"] in width and of a height in proportion to their width. There must be two straight fences 1 m. 60 in height. There may not be more than two or three double jumps, or one double and one treble. The length of the course depends on the size of the stadium. It must not exceed 1,000 metres. The speed required is 400 metres a minute. Exceeding the time limit is penalized by a quarter of a mark . . . Table A scoring is used, with disobediences, falls and obstacles knocked down to be penalized.

Pat Smythe was already touring internationally with the British jumping team in 1948. She was selected for the Olympic team in 1952, but since rules were not changed to permit women to compete, the coach asked for her favorite horse instead. Smythe's chance finally came in 1956, when the gate to Olympic jumping was opened to women.

Smythe, one of the first two women to ride in Olympic jumping, always wore a white carnation in her lapel. Interviewed shortly before her death in 1996, Smythe said, "I love Spain, and I play the guitar. I liked to wear flowers in my hair, so it seemed like a good idea to wear one when I jumped. The carnation was the only flower tough enough."

Smythe herself had to be tough, not only to make it to the Olympic level, but to deal with the blows life dealt her. Both of her parents were dead by the time she was twenty-two, and like her father, Smythe developed severe arthritis when she was in her thirties. The last ten years of her life were compromised by heart disease, made worse because she postponed a much-needed operation to nurse her husband through his final painful years battling cancer.

After Smythe's father died in 1945, her mother, given the choice between keeping the comfortable family home in Crickley or the jumpers with which Pat was beginning to enjoy success, left the family manse and moved the two of them to a boarding house in Bath. The mother and daughter started a riding school and worked hard to maintain themselves and their horses.

The jumper with which Smythe first distinguished herself was Finality, the orphaned offspring of a cart horse. Finality had been rescued and bottle-fed by a friend, then turned over to the Smythes for their care and training.

Finality and Smythe gained experience during World War II in the gymkhanas (informal games competitions) and pony club shows held to raise funds for the Red Cross. The courses at these shows were anything anyone could rig up, and not at all like the sophisticated jumpers of today would be expected to face. At one show, Smythe wrote that she lost the open jumping

Kathy Kusner and Untouchable prepare for departure for a tour of European shows, then and now considered essential for the preparation of Olympic-level competitors. Photo: Courtesy of Kathy Kusner.

class but won musical chairs. Smythe, at age eighteen, enjoyed enough success at the county shows to be invited to ride on the Continent with the British Show Jumping Team. After the "backyard" jumps at the gymkhanas, the courses she encountered on that tour in 1947 were quite a change. As Kathy Kusner, who represented the United States in grand prix jumping in the 1964, 1968, and 1972 Olympics, put it, "When we went to Europe and saw the courses, we thought we were going to die."

From the turn of the century onward, European shows featured banks, ditches, large hedges, water jumps, and every manner of colorful obstacle, often bedecked with flowers. The jump courses were set in large grassy arenas in park-like settings.

Even though she had never faced such challenges, Smythe was quite successful in her debut with the British team. The following season, she and Finality were winning all over England. This sweet winning streak came to a sudden halt when Finality's owner, the man who had taken her as an orphan, sold her.

Finality was a sensitive mare that required a rider with very good hands. Smythe said, "She wouldn't take any bossing or bullying." The new owners had little success with her, but when Smythe again rode her at White City (the entries had been posted before the sale), she and Finality placed second in the King George V Cup (a class closed to women after that year). Finality was sold again, and the new owners permitted Smythe to ride her at Harringay, where Finality was leading show jumper. Initially, the new owners agreed to let Smythe take Finality on the international tour with the British team, but reneged at the last minute because their son wanted to enter the local hunter trials (he did not win).

The same year that Finality was sold, Smythe and her mother again left their house at Crickley, to which they had returned after years in boarding houses. However, the pair were never down long. For less than $500 each, they purchased Tosca, a grey mare considered very difficult to ride, and Prince Hal, a failed steeplechase horse. Within two years, both horses were winning, and mother and daughter were comfortably settled in Miserden, running a guest house.

Then, on January 14, 1952, Smythe's mother was killed when her Jeep went out of control on an icy road and flipped over. Pat was left to cope completely on her own. She had to sell Leona, the third in her string of jumpers.

Undefeated by fate, she continued to show and win with the horses for whom her mother had sacrificed so much. Smythe earned a place on the British Olympic team that same year but was sidelined by FEI rules.

She was asked to lend the team her best horse, Prince Hal, which she did. Prince Hal was a large, high-strung, and strong Thoroughbred, "the best athlete I ever owned," Smythe said.

Prince Hal wanted to race at his fences, but if he ran away, he would refuse, shrieking to a stop right at the jump. "He would frighten himself," Smythe said. "I was strong, and it took that to ride him, but I was also very accurate, and he trusted me to put him at just the right spot to jump each time."

The team coach had no luck with her horse. Hal would not jump for other riders. Smythe said that when Prince Hal was returned, he was thin and nervous, and his self-confidence so shaken that it took months of patient reschooling before he returned to his previous form.

In spite of the near-miss with the Olympics and the deplorable condition of her horse after his months with the team, Smythe complained only about being barred from the 1954 World Jumping Championship. Smythe had sent off her entries, assumed they had been accepted since she heard nothing different, and shipped horses to Spain. Though the FEI rules had been revised to permit women to ride in Olympic jumping, she learned through an off-hand remark after arriving in Spain that another FEI rule had been passed barring women from riding in the World Championship.

The FEI rules were quirky. Women, who had shown internationally for decades, were not allowed to ride on their Nation's Cup teams in Europe until 1952. Michele Cancre rode for France, and Janine Mahieu for Belgium at Rome that year, and Smythe represented Great Britain at White City, England.

The Prix des Nations, or Nation's Cup, is a team event. According to FEI rule 102, Article II, 1953, the purpose of the competition is to measure the efficiency of the riders of different nations. Four riders represent each team, and competitors jump the same course twice. This is the competition that determines the team jumping medals at the Olympics. The Nation's Cup is considered the climax of the show, and riding for one's nation is a highly coveted position.

When women were finally permitted to ride in the 1956 Olympics at Stockholm, Smythe thought, "Thank goodness, I'll finally get a stab at it."

A second woman, Brigitte Schockaert, who represented Belgium, also rode in 1956. Schockaert collected 59 faults over the unusually difficult Olympic course.

Smythe said that Prince Hal hadn't won her many good points with the team coach. The coach didn't like her or her uncooperative horses, so when she finally got her chance to ride in the Olympics, she was informed she would have to do so without Prince Hal. With Prince Hal, she had set the Ladies' High Jump record for Europe at 7'4½", and won many international and grand prix classes. In fact, Prince Hal had won every single Puissance class in which he was entered—these classes feature increasingly shorter courses and bigger fences until one competitor alone can clear the height. To win, Prince Hal twice cleared 7'3".

Even with all these credentials, the team coach would have nothing of the horse that had so vexed him four years earlier. Instead, Smythe would ride Flanagan, a "common little Irish horse with just one year of international experience."

Flanagan had been purchased in Ireland by Brigadier Lyndon Bolton, an Englishman. Bolton spotted the stocky, slightly Roman-nosed little horse grazing in a herd of fine, young Thoroughbreds. Flanagan, the farmer explained, lived on a poor plot several farms way, but jumped over numerous walls to upgrade his grazing and his companions. Bolton brought Flanagan home with him to England.

The Olympic course at Stockholm was immense, with two awkwardly strided combinations. To add to the riders' miseries, heavy thunderstorms hit twice during the week leading up to the grand prix jumping, and rain poured the morning of competition as riders readied their mounts for the fearsome test.

The worst problem for Smythe and the game Flanagan was an in-and-out, the "in" an oxer 4'7" and almost 5 feet wide, the "out" an oxer 4'9" by 5'7" with 29 feet in between the two jumps. The standard distance for an in-and-out with one stride between fences is 24 to 26 feet, for two strides, about 36 feet. Meeting two gigantic oxers with such a distance in between was mission impossible for Flanagan. There is a photograph of Flanagan diving down over the outermost pole, with Smythe straining to give the horse his head. He caught the pole between his legs, and how he righted himself for the rest of the course, Smythe could not imagine. He had only one other knockdown—at the tricky triple combination—for a round total of 8 faults.

This put Great Britain in second place going into round two. The sun improved the footing for round two, and Flanagan tried his utmost, this time stretching and somehow clearing the difficult double. The pair were clean riding into the final triple combination, but here things went wrong. Flanagan had checked slightly after the 16'4½" water jump, met the five-foot wall on a short stride, and could not get up momentum for the large oxer leading into the triple. By the time they got through that combination, the pair had picked up 13 faults, tenth best of sixty-six starters. The British team finished third.

Pat Smythe, the first woman to ride in the Olympics, always wore a white carnation. She won a team bronze medal aboard Flanagan in 1956. Flanagan tried his heart out at Stockholm, but Smythe said the Olympic course was beyond his scope. Photo: Jean Bridel, L'Année Hippique; courtesy of the family of Pat Smythe.

"Flanagan had all sorts of character, and he tried his heart out, but the Olympic course was too much for him. The jumps were so big and the distances between fences so long that the course suited the big, powerful German horses. Prince Hal (a tall horse with a long stride) could have bounded over the course. I think he could have won the gold medal, given a chance," Smythe said. The Germans won both the team and individual gold medals.

After her efforts in the Olympics, she received the Order of the British Empire (OBE), awarded by HRH Queen Elizabeth to those who are both outstanding in their fields and excellent ambassadors for Great Britain.

Smythe, OBE, and Flanagan, BIH (brave Irish horse!) tried again in 1960 at the Rome Olympics, finishing eleventh in the individual ranking. In those days, the rules called for only three riders in the Nation's Cup, and all three had to finish for the team's score to count. Dawn Palethorpe Wofford (wife of J.E.B. Wofford, who rode for the United States in 1952), one of Great Britain's four riders, was left on the sidelines in favor of a man, who was eliminated, thus eliminating the team.

Smythe's career with the British team lasted twenty years. In 1963, she married Sam Koechlin, a Swiss three-day rider. The couple were the parents of two daughters, and between family life and two hip replacements, Smythe's jumping career came to an end. She had won four European Ladies' Championships, eight British National Championships, and been part of thirteen winning Nation's Cup teams. Fortunately, her writing career continued. Smythe's horses and riding career are well documented through her books, as is the history of show jumping. Her autobiographies (written in 1956 and 1992) are inspirational for both youths and adults.

At the time she was interviewed for this book, Smythe was recovering from a heart attack—her "sixth, seventh, or eighth." Her voice was very frail, but her will and sense of humor remained intact. She was tickled because *Horse and Hound,* Britain's most popular weekly horse journal, had run a photo of her on the cover. Smythe assumed the magazine was running her obituary. "I thought, I am still here, I have beaten them again." When she looked inside the magazine, she learned the article was actually about Prince Hal, featured in the magazine's "Horses of a Lifetime" series. Sadly, her actual obituary followed, much too quickly. Smythe died at age 68, only weeks later, but to the end she remained the toughest flower.

★ ★ ★ ★

In the United States, the army provided all the members of the Olympic riding teams between 1912 and 1948. When the cavalry was officially disbanded after the 1948 Olympics, open trials were held for a civilian team at Ft. Riley, Kansas, site of the Army's former Cavalry School. Riders came from all parts of the country, including a number of women.

Prior to the trials, civilian jumping in America most often consisted of courses of four jumps, twice around. Faults were given if a jump was touched; whereas, FEI rules penalize only jumps that are knocked down. The emphasis in America, therefore, was on jumping clean. Little variety was found in the obstacles encountered, with few spread fences or combinations and hardly any timed classes. Competitors would soar over one fence, often clearing it

Rocksie and Margaret Cotter, shown jumping a six-foot fence in 1938, exemplify the style prevalent in the United States before civilians rode over the international courses of the Olympics. Photo: Thomas Neil Darling; courtesy of Howard Allen.

by a foot, take time to reorganize, and then face the next fence when ready. Jumper classes were usually held in tanbark arenas. Permanent obstacles could not be employed, because following the jumping, the arena was cleared for classes featuring fine-harness horses and saddle horses.

Most of the riders in the open jumping division before 1950 were professionals, and almost all of them were males who made their living showing and selling horses. There were a few women who did well in the open classes, but they were exceptions. Two such women were Betty Bosley Bird, who claimed the Professional Horseman's Trophy over forty-six men in 1947, and Margaret Cotter. Cotter and her horse Rocksie won the Jumper Championship at the New York National in 1941. Back then, taking the jumper championship at Madison Square Garden was the equivalent of winning the national championship. Such women were tolerated in varying degrees by the pros. Since women usually rode only their own horses, they were not considered a threat by most of the pros. Some women who showed jumpers, though, remember being criticized "for interfering with men who were trying to make a living."

Many more women rode in the hunter ranks, and they did well. Jumpers had only to clear obstacles, in whatever style, but the hunters, expensive and perfectly formed, were judged on style of jumping, manners, and grace of movement. Special hunter classes were held for lady riders. Corinthian classes, ridden wearing full hunting regalia, and hunt team classes were limited to amateurs, giving women ample opportunity to show. Among the most successful at the National Horse Show from the 1930s to the 1950s were Betty Perry (the first of two Bettys to be married to William Haggin Perry and known for this distinction as "B One"), Liz Whitney Tippett, Mrs. John McDonald, Mrs. Thomas Waller, Peggy Steinman, Sally Wheeler, Ellie Wood Keith Baxter, Joan Walsh, and Joan Boyce (the latter two also rode jumpers).

In the early days, women who showed at the Garden were required to ride sidesaddle. It was not until the teens, when this rule was slackened, that women won in open competition against men. The first woman to show astride at the National Horse Show was Marion du Pont Scott, who rode in a ladies' saddle horse class in 1915. She won her class and came back that night to win again, this time riding sidesaddle. The press said little about the well-born Miss du Pont, but when a young Canadian, Elisabeth Coulthard, rode astride over fences in a ladies' hunter class later during the same show, she drew criticism; although, the young men at the Garden that night "applauded her efforts violently." During the same time period, Mrs. Jean Austin du Pont won many hunter classes riding sidesaddle and was said to jump "six-foot fences with aplomb."

Liz Whitney Tippett, here on Grey Knight, was famous for her homebred grey hunters. Photo: Thomas Neil Darling; courtesy of Howard Allen.

Such is the background of showing in America prior to the USET trial in 1950. This seemed to put women at a terrible disadvantage when asked to face an international style course, but Capt. Jack Fritz, secretary of the USET, said, "All civilians were at a disadvantage in those days, not just women."

Proving Fritz's point, two women, Carol Durand and Norma Matthews, were chosen to be on the first USET jumping team.

Durand hailed from Kansas City, not far from Ft. Riley. As an honorary member of the Ft. Riley fox hunt, she might have come in contact with the international-style obstacles on the cavalry training grounds there; though Dana Durand, Mrs. Durand's widower, said his wife never got to train with the army during their heyday. She learned to ride as a little girl under the

Ellie Wood Keith Baxter and Shawnee Farm's Kentucky show the good form over the big outside courses at the Warrenton Horse Show. Photo: Courtesy of The Fauquier Times-Democrat.

instruction of an excellent Irish horseman who taught at the country club in Kansas City. During grade school, Durand moved to New Mexico, where she rode at a ranch that had Thoroughbreds, not the more usual cow ponies. After that, Durand started showing on the West Coast. Jump courses in California were more sophisticated than those found elsewhere in the nation, perhaps because the 1932 Olympics were held there, Olympian William Steinkraus speculated.

Durand took advantage of diverse opportunities to gain as much riding experience as possible—she galloped horses for the great trainer Ben Jones and worked with her friend Shirley Drew Hardwick, a saddle horse trainer, to develop the riding program at Stephens College.

With notable exceptions, jumping activity in America clung to the shorelines, either in California or along the Atlantic. During Durand's day, though, there lingered a collection of very good hunters and jumpers clustered around Ft. Riley, Kansas City, and St. Louis. The jumper division at the American Royal at Kansas City was among the tops in the country.

"The horsemen from the Midwest thought Carol Durand was the best living jumping rider," recalled Steinkraus, Durand's teammate in 1951. Demonstrating this faith, owners provided Durand with excellent mounts. Durand was named to ride Reno Kirk, one of the army horses leased by the USET, and Miss Budweiser, the best jumper of the day. Miss Budweiser won the 1950 jumper championship at New York under the name of Circus Rose, before being purchased for Durand to ride and renamed by Augustus Busch of St. Louis.

In 1950, Carol Durand and Norma Matthews represented the USET on the indoor circuit with Arthur McCashin, the sole male on the team. The following year, a *New York Tribune* article noted that the 1951 USET squad included three men along with Durand, unlike the 1950 team, which had only one man along with the women.

The late Arthur McCashin, Durand's teammate from 1950 through 1953, was also one of her best friends. Together, they racked up an unprecedented number of wins, while showing in the pairs jumping classes that were still contested back then.

"There were few spread fences in American horse shows before 1950, and no timed classes," said Mr. Durand, who himself served as a committee member and steward at many of the shows in those days. "With the FEI classes starting in 1950, the riders had to learn to gallop over a fence."

It didn't take either Durand or McCashin long to catch on to the new style. They were always watching and learning, according to Kathi Fordyce, who worked for both. When the USET went to Europe, Durand and

Norma Matthews, aboard her unique Paint, Country Boy, Arthur McCashin on Pale-face and Carol Durand on Reno Kirk (reserve horse, 1952 Olympics) rode on the 1950 Fall Indoor Circuit as the first USET jumping team. Photo: Courtesy of Dr. Fred McCashin.

McCashin studied the courses and watched international riders schooling horses. Once back in the United States, Durand and McCashin were setting up schooling fences and the lines of combinations they had seen in Europe, then adapting and refining these methods for their own use.

When time came for the 1952 Olympics, Durand made the team. Her husband said, "Back then, there was a trial. The top four riders were selected, and Carol was one of those."

There was doubt as to whether she could ride, though, because FEI rules still forbade women from riding in the Olympics. The FEI relaxed their ban and permitted women to ride in dressage in 1952, but not in jumping or the three-day. Both of Durand's horses had been shipped to Europe, and McCashin rode Miss Budweiser in the Olympics, achieving the best score of the

Americans, finishing 12th. Her other mount, Reno Kirk, was the squad's reserve horse.

"I have no doubt Carol would have done admirably had she been permitted to ride at Helsinki," said Steinkraus. The USET, with Steinkraus, McCashin, and Col. John Russell, an army rider who had ridden in the 1948 Olympics, won the team bronze.

Durand's husband, her friends, and McCashin's family do not recall any particular disappointment or bitterness on her part at having missed the Olympics. Sitting on the sidelines was pretty much a woman's plight at that time.

Durand rode for USET again in 1953 and was part of the team to win the Nation's Cup at Harrisburg. The squad won eight team victories for the fall, and she won the International Individual Championship at the New York National.

In 1953, the FEI rules finally changed to permit women to ride in the grand prix jumping at the Olympics. Durand, however, dropped off the squad after that year.

"Riding on the team and traveling to the different horse shows took so much time," Fordyce said. "I think she felt she had spent too much time away from her young son and husband already. I think she wanted to stay home with her family."

Then, too, Durand's interest had always lain with finding horses and developing them. McCashin's son Fred, who is now a veterinarian in Southern Pines, North Carolina, agreed this love pulled Durand away from international jumping. Fred McCashin said, "Carol would find horses and bring them East to show, and leave them with my father. Or she would spot a horse she liked, and Dad would go out to Kansas to look at it and bring it back."

Her husband said, "She ate, slept, and breathed horses. She could spot a good one a mile off. She never stuck with one too long—she knew what they could do, started them, sold them, and moved along. She was very good at matching the right horse with a rider."

In 1971, Durand suffered an untimely death while checking out one of these prospects at a racetrack. She hopped on the horse to try it out, and the horse reared over backwards, crushing her against the race track rail.

The other woman who rode for the team in 1950 was Norma Matthews, who came from Sacramento, California. She was described by the national press as "a pretty blue-eyed blonde, 5'6½", 125 pounds." The newspapers might have been describing a candidate for Miss America, instead of an international-caliber athlete.

Steinkraus remembered that Matthews' horse for the trials was the unique skewbald (brown and white) Country Boy. "He was one of the first warm-bloods on the team," Steinkraus said wryly. He was big and heavy compared with the other team horses, which were Thoroughbred or near Thorough-bred, but Country Boy, all 17 hands, 1,450-pounds of him, could jump. Country Boy's limiting factor was his aversion to ditches and water jumps. Steinkraus said the horse was wall-eyed and that horses with this defect (a light blue iris resulting from lack of brown pigment) sometimes perceive things like water in a different manner. Still, Matthews and Country Boy helped account for twenty ribbons and five wins in international jumping classes in the autumn of 1950.

After Durand and Matthews, no American women came forward to try for the team until Kathy Kusner in 1958. A year earlier, Kusner wrote the USET to find out what was required to try out for the team. The reply was hardly encouraging. First, she was informed that she was too small. Women riders in those days had to carry 154 pounds in competition, meaning the petite Kusner would have to make up the difference with a heavy lead pad. Second, the Olympic courses were long and difficult. Kusner's respondent questioned if a woman would be strong enough for the task, overlooking the many successes women had already achieved in international jumping. None-theless, an invitation was extended to Kusner to participate in trials in 1958, from which riders would be selected to train for the 1960 Olympics.

When asked if she felt that there was hostility toward women at the 1958 trials, Kusner said no; while she was a great advocate of racial equality, gender equality was not something she had given much thought. Any inequality she sensed when she arrived for the trials at Greenwich, Connecticut was due to her own lack of polish compared with that of the other candidates, who were very sophisticated. Like Kusner, Pat Smythe said the "woman question" had always caught her by surprise, too. Smythe said when she was riding, she never thought of herself as a woman, only as a competitor.

Smythe had grown up in horse-loving England. Her mother rode, and Smythe had a pony from age three. Kusner, on the other hand, grew up in the suburbs with non-horsey parents. Nonetheless, Kusner really wanted to ride, and she begged for a horse. If only her parents would buy the horse, she would work to support it. At age twelve, her parents relented and bought her a pony. True to her promise, Kusner earned money for feed and supplies by hawking pony rides in her East Falls Church, Virginia, neighborhood. Her father built the pony a shelter in the backyard and later rigged up a home-made trailer so Kusner could take riding lessons.

Kusner had seen a poster advertising a horse show at Bailey's Cross Roads. On the appointed day, she rode over to see what it was all about and, to her surprise, learned that the competitors rode in saddles and used bridles with multiple reins (full bridles and pelhams). Kusner, who had only ridden bareback, was intrigued. She asked how she might learn this unique form of riding and was pointed toward Jane Marshall Dillon, who taught many of the best young riders of the day at the Junior Equitation School.

From then on, her father would haul Kusner and her pony to Mrs. Dillon's in Alexandria on Saturday mornings and pick them up on Sunday evenings. Kusner said, "Mrs. Dillon provided such a wholesome environment. It was so much fun being there."

She took lessons from Mrs. Dillon, who was a disciple of Capt. Vladimir Littauer, one of the masters of forward seat riding. In return, Kusner helped train the school ponies and performed stable duty. "My post, years later, was held by Joe Fargis," Kusner reported proudly. Fargis was to win the individual and team jumping gold medals at the 1984 Olympics in Los Angeles.

Kusner would go to horse shows with Mrs. Dillon's crew. At the Harrisburg National in 1956 while traveling as the groom of April Dawn, the Junior Equitation School's best, Kusner first saw the USET team. "It was too good to be true," Kusner said, remembering the moment. She thought the team was perfection—so beautifully turned out, so stylish in their execution of the difficult international courses. "From that moment on, I had a dream and a goal—to ride on the team, though I had no idea how to go about it."

Kusner was by then riding horses for professional dealers, which gave her plenty of experience jumping, and jumping under the watchful eye of some of the best horsemen of the day. She blended the rough-and-ready techniques of the pros with the refined style taught by Mrs. Dillon.

Women, particularly women like Kusner who could "catch ride" (ride a strange horse without practice), were often asked to show in the ladies' classes and other hunter classes restricted to amateurs. Between 1956 and 1958, Kusner rode in many horse shows and showed some of the best horses in the country. She would also try her luck on jumpers when given the chance—in fact, she would ride anything.

Among the top owners for whom she rode was Mrs. Theodora Randolph. Mrs. Randolph bred and raised her own hunters, and hers were some of the best. Kusner confided in Mrs. Randolph that she longed to try out for the USET.

Mrs. Randolph, who could spot a good horse and also a good rider, was all for it. Together they selected High Noon, a palomino Kusner was showing for a horse dealer, and Mrs. Randolph purchased the horse for Kusner to take to the trials. Kusner said, "High Noon was not exactly an international-level jumper, but he was the obvious choice from the scruffy lot of jumpers that I was riding at the time. Mrs. Randolph also helped select and purchased for me better riding clothes for the trials."

At the trials, Kusner and Mary Litchfield were invited to train that winter with Bertalan de Nemethy. Nemethy, a Hungarian who came to this country to train horses for Eleonora Sears, was hired by the USET team in 1955. A major rebuilding campaign was required since the supply of cavalry horses had dried up and the number of cavalry-trained riders was diminishing. Before 1955, the team had enjoyed some early success utilizing talented horses brought from Europe after World War II, the best they could scrounge

Bertalan de Nemethy taught classic style during his many successful years as coach of the USET jumping team. Photo: Louisa Woodville, The Fauquier Times-Democrat.

from the domestic open jumper circuit, and some very good but ancient cavalry horses leased in 1950. Nemethy had the skills and basis in classical equitation and international competition needed for the team.

As a European, Nemethy did not come from a tradition of women riders, but Emily, his wife, remembered, "When he saw Kathy, he knew what he had."

When Nemethy began coaching the USET team, he looked at the hodge-podge of styles of the riders and took every rider back to basics, longeing them (driving the horses around him on a long line) without stirrups end-lessly to achieve proper position.

Kusner said, "It was necessary for me to learn a more neutral base in order to ride the big international courses, opposed to the very forward seat that was being taught in America at the time."

Kusner trained the winter of 1958 and 1959 with Nemethy, and then yet another miracle occurred. Following the 1960 Olympics and fall circuit, George Morris, a member of the silver medal–winning jumping squad, re-tired from riding to become an actor. Kusner was named to ride Sinjon, on whom Morris had placed fourth in the Rome Olympics.

"It was too good to be true. When I used to help groom and braid the team horses, Sinjon was one of my favorites. Now, I was going to get to ride him. I couldn't believe it—I was so grateful, I set out to be the perfect pupil, to do everything exactly as Bert had taught me," Kusner said.

Kusner threw out everything she had learned before, all the natural instincts that earned her an opportunity with the USET in the first place. Kusner said she became completely wooden, unable to give the sensitive Thoroughbred the ride he deserved. Sinjon went into the first and only slump of his brilliant career.

"I couldn't do anything right. Amazingly, in spite of my bad perfor-mances, they took me to Europe in 1962. Sinjon had been reassigned to Billy Steinkraus, and was back winning again. I tried even harder to be perfect, and got even worse. I began to think, 'The problem is, I'm not good enough. I just don't have the talent.'"

At Dublin, at the end of the tour and what Kusner was certain was the end of her career with the USET, she decided to ride High Noon in her old style and, as a result, finished second in two important time classes, coming within a fraction of a second of winning both.

That winter, she worked to combine the classical style she had been taught and the skills she had learned schooling and showing numerous horses for dealers. These factors, blended with her natural instincts and feel, pro-vided the key to her long and winning career with the USET.

Kusner said she took acting classes years later. She found out acting was very technical, and the class worked endlessly on techniques, but when the students actually performed, they were told to forget everything they had learned, and just follow instinct. For Kusner, riding was like that. She said, "The technique becomes natural and part of you. You don't have time to think about it—especially when you're riding against the clock." Kusner, who is also a jet-rated pilot, said, "Riding an international course is like flying an airplane: you always have to be planning what you need to do next while you're taking care of the needs of the moment."

Kusner first represented the USET in 1961. The following year, two more women, Mary Mairs and Carol Hofmann, got their chance, too. George Morris and Hugh Wiley, two members of the ultra-strong 1960 Olympic squad, dropped off the team, which left two berths open for the 1964 games in Tokyo. Mairs and Kusner were asked to join Steinkraus, who had ridden in every previous Olympics since 1952, and Frank Chapot, who had ridden in 1956 and 1960.

The 1964 squad finished 6th. Kusner, on her most successful horse, Untouchable, was thirteenth over all, with Mairs thirty-third. The same team went to Mexico City in 1968. Here, Steinkraus won the individual gold in a competition held on a separate day from the Nation's Cup. Unfortunately, Steinkraus's mount, Snowbound, could not show with the team in the Prix des Nations, so it was up to Kusner, Mairs (who was now Mrs. Frank Chapot), and Mr. Frank Chapot. The course was the most difficult since 1956—more so, in fact—the team that won had over 100 faults. All three members of the USET somehow survived, finishing fourth.

At that Olympics, Marion Coakes (now Mrs. David Mould), riding pint-sized Stroller, a 14.2-hand Irish pony, claimed the individual silver, representing Great Britain. Coakes had ridden the game little Stroller to many successes as a junior, including the Junior European Championships in 1962. She and Stroller won the first Ladies' World Championships in 1965, and sports writers named Coakes Sportswoman of the Year. In 1968, Coakes became the first woman to claim an individual Olympic jumping medal. Her long string of international wins aboard Stroller continued through 1971. In 1972, another young British woman, Anne Moore, also straight out of junior ranks, repeated Coakes' success and claimed the individual silver in 1972 at Munich. Her mount was Psalm, only a little taller than Stroller and more slightly built.

In Munich, Kusner stood on the podium to receive a team silver, only $\frac{1}{4}$ fault behind the gold medalists. By 1972, Mrs. Chapot had dropped off the team to start a family. She had risen to the USET through the

Marion Coakes and pony-sized Stroller were stars of the 1968 Olympics, winning the individual silver medal. Photo: Courtesy of The Chronicle of the Horse.

horsemanship ranks, claiming both the ASPCA Maclay and AHSA Medal. Tomboy, the horse that had carried her to these victories, was also her mount for international competition. Mrs. Chapot wrote, "Tomboy had a very quiet disposition and great confidence in herself . . . I shall always be grateful to Tomboy for the generous way in which she introduced me to show jumping at the highest level. It was only on other horses that I ever learned how difficult some of those courses really were!"

Chapot rode mostly family-owned horses, rather than team horses, and she rode them with the same smoothness she had used to win her horsemanship medals. An admirer said, "I was sorry when Mary quit the team. She was a beautiful rider with impeccable style. She made it look so easy. She was neat to watch and especially good with nervous horses. Frank [Chapot] was a rough and ready kind of guy who could get the job done. Their daughter Laura rides with the graceful style of her mother." (Laura has enjoyed great success on the grand prix circuit aboard Gem Twist, sired by Good Twist, on whom her father earned so many victories in international competition.)

Kusner continued to ride on the team through 1976. During the years between 1961 and 1976, she accumulated enough first place wins in major international classes, the Olympics, the Pan American Games (team gold, 1963), Nation's Cups, and the Fall Indoor Circuit to fill two pages of a legal notebook. She is the first woman to have ridden in three consecutive Olympics and was Ladies' European Champion and second in the Ladies' World Championship.

Kusner said, "When I first started traveling with the team, at shows I would go into the parking lot and see who had the nicest vans. Then I would judge the tack rooms and the tack. I would see what the horses were fed and how they were cared for. I tried to watch all the big riders school their horses. When we had free time, I would follow Billy [Steinkraus] and Bert [de Nemethy] around to the museums and cultural attractions. I wouldn't know if the church we visited was Gothic or Romanesque style, but they would tell me and explain the history and art that was involved also. After eleven years, I knew what all the horses ate and could lead sight-seeing tours of every city we visited. I was interested in learning about new things and wanted to concentrate more on race riding."

So, it was left to other American women to be the first to claim the Olympic gold. Another British woman, Debbie Johnsey, made it into the jump-off for the silver medal at Montreal in 1976, but finished fourth. No American women rode in Olympic jumping that year, which came as a big disappointment for Melanie Smith.

Smith had set her sights on the Olympic team during her pony club days. Smith said, "It didn't seem like a realistic dream at the time, but I figured I should set my goals as high as possible and do the best I could."

The goal seemed within reach in 1976, when the horse she was riding at the time, Radnor II, was the leading money winner on the grand prix circuit. She remembered, "I tried out for the team that would tour Europe in 1976. Seven riders tried for six spots. They sat us down in a room, read the list of riders who had made the team—every one's name but mine—and then asked me to leave the room so they could plan for the trip."

Smith's riding career began at age three on the family horse and pony farm in Germantown, Tennessee. Her mother taught riding, and Melanie's mount would lead the classes through their paces. She also freshened up the school mounts when they became uncooperative.

Smith said, "Until I was three I didn't want to be around the horses at all, which had my mother worried. After that, though, I was on horseback for hours every day. It was a wonderful childhood.

"The only instruction I had, other than from my mother, was through the pony club, which I really enjoyed. Then in 1968, Mother and I drove the purple station wagon and trailer across the state to Knoxville for a George Morris clinic. I asked if I could come and ride with him, and he said politely that I had a plain bay horse that was nothing special, and he didn't think so. The following year we were back for his clinic—same question—and this time, he asked the two of us what we hoped to accomplish. My mother said without hesitation, 'I want Melanie to ride in the Olympics.' I think that surprised and rather fascinated George. He said vaguely that maybe we could join him in Florida."

"That winter, we drove the purple station wagon to Florida, and while George was very nice, I can't say he paid a bit of attention to us. Then, in the first show I entered, my horse, The Irishman, won the amateur-owner jumper championship, and George became more interested. Actually, I won the amateur-owner championship at every show in which I rode that year. By May, George said maybe we should think about making The Irishman the AHSA year-end champion, and I said, 'That sounds great. What's that?' He was awfully surprised that the horse had never been registered with the AHSA and had not gotten a single point for all of his wins. The Irishman did, however, become AHSA champion, even though we didn't get credit for any points won until May."

After the Florida shows, Morris did everything he could to help. He never charged Smith for lessons, letting her work them off by braiding, grooming, and teaching. It was Morris who found sponsors for the horses that carried Smith the rest of the way to the Olympics. Through Morris, she met and became friends with the Neil Eustaces. The Eustaces wanted to buy a jumper for Smith to ride, so they all went to Europe and picked out Val de Loire, an experienced jumper with a "stop" in him, and Calypso, a green (inexperienced) horse.

With these two horses came honors (Horse of the Year, Rider of the Year, Woman Rider of the Year) with enough consistency that she was not denied a spot on the 1980 Olympic squad. The only problem was that President Jimmy Carter ordered an Olympics boycott.

Smith said, "It was very frustrating, but of course we supported the political decision our country made." She rode on the team in the Alternate Olympics in Rotterdam. The USET placed fifth, represented by Smith and two other women, Katie Monahan and Terry Rudd, and Norman Dello Joio. Smith was tied for the individual gold, but finished third after riding first in the jump-off, a disadvantage because time is the determining factor if no jumping faults are incurred.

Like the United States, most other jumping powers also boycotted the Moscow Olympics and competed instead in Rotterdam. Smith said, "I felt vindicated for 1976. I won major competitions in Rome, Ireland, and England while touring with the team in 1980."

Even so, Smith was afraid she was again going to be the rider sent out of the room when the team was announced for 1984. Team coach Bert de Nemethy had retired. Frank Chapot served as chef d' equipe (to aid the team with entries and so on), but not as team coach in the sense Nemethy had, who trained a group of horses and riders, then named the team from these. Riders were to be selected by a committee through observation trials. In these, another woman, Leslie Burr, clearly had the best record. Smith, Joe Fargis, Conrad Homfeld, and Anne Kursinski all had records that were comparable. These five riders were named to the team, but no one was named alternate. A week before the Olympics, the five rode in the Friendly Games.

"These should have been called the unfriendly games," Smith observed. Rather than using the event as it was intended—to give competitors a chance to let their horses have a look at the Olympic arena and jumps—the USET members were riding for their lives. Smith tied for first, but even so, she wasn't certain she would make the team. Smith said, "It was Anne Kursinski whom they asked to leave the room. I felt awfully sorry for her. I'm glad she has since gotten her chance [1988, 1992 and 1996]."

Frank Chapot, after riding in six Olympics, was for the first time team coach. He wrote that the first problem was to select the five from among a dozen very good candidates, then to choose four for the team competition, then three for the individual competition. Smith made both cuts. She was seventh in the individual competition, behind teammates Joe Fargis, who won the gold, and Conrad Homfeld, who won the silver. The strain of the selection process was also acknowledged by the two medal winners when interviewed after the Games. The bronze medal winner was Heidi Robbiani, the only other woman who rode in the jumping that year besides Smith and Leslie Burr.

The boycott had denied Smith her place in Olympic annals when she claimed her bronze medal in 1980, but she and Burr earned their place in history in 1984 when they became the first women to receive Olympic gold medals in the team jumping.

When the great day came, it wasn't as Smith had dreamed years ago in pony club. She said, "I always cared about riding on the team, not as an

The high-strung Albany was upset by the huge crowd at Los Angeles, but Leslie Burr steadied him to put the United States in position for its first team gold in Olympic jumping competition. Burr made it to her second Olympics in 1996. Photo: John Strassburger, The Chronicle of the Horse.

individual. I wanted that feeling we used to have in pony club when all members were working for the team score."

The American riders came together for that one day as talented individuals. Until the team competition, all had ridden against one another as arch rivals. Any hopes of true cohesion among team members were lost because of the method by which the team was selected. Now the USET is using a points system at designated events as the basis for choosing a team. This system, too, has its faults, but Smith said, "At least everyone knows where they stand."

By whatever selection process used, American women have always been well represented since the advent of civilian teams. Smith did not try for the team again after 1984. She had accomplished what she set out to do and moved back to Memphis in 1987 to help her father, as her mother slipped into the early stages of Alzheimer's. As a very happy side note, Smith, at age thirty-nine and with nothing further from her mind, suddenly walked up on the love of her life at a local polo match in 1988. Smith and Lee Taylor were married that Christmas, and "life just keeps getting better every day."

The USET's silver medal–winning team at Seoul in 1988 included Anne Kursinski (tied for fourth individually) and Lisa Jacquin. Both of these women again rode for America at Barcelona in 1992. This time the team placed fifth.

Gold medalist Steinkraus mused, "Will a woman ever win the individual gold medal at the Olympics? Yes, I think it's just a matter of time, rather than skill.

"However, special factors are involved. The Olympics come only once every four years, and the courses have tended to be harder than any other you have to face during those forty-eight months.

"Winning the gold medal is like grabbing the brass ring. It takes the right horse, the right course, and the right day. On their day, the best women riders are certainly capable of winning anything, anywhere. But partly it's a matter of numbers, too. Many more men than women get to ride in the Olympics, which puts the numbers against them," Steinkraus concluded.

Eventing—Fearing the Worst,
Achieving the Best

BILL ROYCROFT'S HARD FALL IN THE 1960 OLYMPICS was used as an excuse for continuing to bar women from the Olympic three-day. Roycroft, a tough as-nails Australian, helped his team win the gold medal that year by remounting and finishing the cross-country course, even though he was half conscious and had broken his collar bone. He went to the hospital but was released so he could ride in the final phase of the event the next day.

Lt. Col. Frank Weldon (British) reportedly said, "Who'd like to be the brave man to do that [require her to finish for the team] to a woman?"

The irony is Weldon's fears about women competing have come true again and again since 1964, the first year women were permitted to ride in the Olympic three-day. Women, as well as men, regularly sustain falls and injuries in this toughest of Olympic horse sports.

American Lana du Pont (now Mrs. W. C. Wright), the first woman to ride in the Olympic three-day, fell twice on the cross-country course at Tokyo in 1964 due to heavy footing and hard rain. Her best friend, Donnan Sharp Monk (formerly married to Michael Plumb), gave her a leg up after the first fall and told her to go on.

Du Pont remembers that her horse fell on her and that her knee hurt badly. She was somewhat dazed but did as her friend told her. Later du Pont

Caroline Treviranus Leake on her mare Cajun, jumping a steeplechase fence in the Advanced Division of the Blue Ridge Hunt Three-Day Event (Virginia). Cajun was USCTA Horse of the Year in 1973. This pair represented the United States at the Burghley (England) World Championships in 1974. Photo: Gamecock.

learned that her horse, Mr. Wister, had broken his lower jaw, an injury that continued to plague him for some time.

Du Pont and Mr. Wister completed the course and jumped the stadium course the following day. She shared a silver medal with her teammates but gave all the credit to "the boys. They were great. I was just along for the ride."

In the 1968 Olympics in Mexico, more women followed Lana's example. Three of Ireland's four riders were women, and Jane Bullen (now Holderness-Roddam), representing Great Britain, was the first woman to win a team gold medal in the three-day.

Bullen had the second best score of her team, in spite of two falls on the cross-country. Like du Pont, she was also the victim of deteriorating weather conditions. Bullen and Our Nobby were upended when rising waters, fed by rains up the valley, obliterated the riveted concrete lips of water jumps.

"Even with two falls, Our Nobby still had the fastest time," Bullen said, as she remembered the ordeal.

Because of the trick nature played on him, Our Nobby retired after the Olympics, suffering a permanent loss of confidence. Even out hunting, Bullen said, "Approaching open water, I had to be very careful. He always remembered."

HRH Princess Anne fell heavily twice on the cross-country course at the 1976 Olympics in Montreal. Blinding rain struck just as she began the 4½ mile cross-country course, and her horse floundered and fell at the 19th fence, perhaps landing on top of her. Princess Anne remembered little, having suffered a concussion, but finishing without another fault.

Lt. Col. Bill Lithgrow, the team's manager, wrote, "In Montreal, a message was sent back that a certain fence was a bit wet and was causing trouble, but it didn't get back in time to warn Princess Anne, and she fell there."

To paraphrase Colonel Weldon, "Who's going to be the royal subject to tell the princess she must continue the course?"

Princess Anne proved her mettle and put eventing on the map. Her performance at Montreal, where she was one of only two on her team to finish the course, demonstrated her courage, and earlier successes in the European Championships—the individual gold in 1971 and individual and team silver in 1975—affirmed her skill. Janet Hodgson, Lucinda Prior-Palmer, and Sue Hatherley were also on the British team in 1975.

Most people were not familiar with three-day eventing until the publicity that surrounded Princess Anne's participation at Montreal. She did other event riders a real favor, because from then on, rather than offer a ten-minute explanation of their sport, they could simply say, "I ride in the three-day, you know, like Princess Anne!"

HRH Princess Anne put eventing on the map and also displayed skill on the race course.

Until the 1950s and 1960s, most horsemen knew no more about the sport than the general public. Through 1948, the three-day was limited to military officers and was referred to as "the military." (Enlisted men were considered professionals and not allowed to ride.) Modern-day aliases for this Olympic discipline include concours complete d'equatation, concours complete, CCI, or three-day eventing. Its abbreviated cousin is the one-day event, or horse trials. Those who participate usually refer to themselves as event riders or eventers.

The three phases of competition included in "the military" were originally designed to prove the mettle of an officer's mount. Day one is dressage, or a programmed ride, which demonstrated the basic obedience of the army mount and ensured his worthy deportment on the parade field. Day two is an endurance test with difficult obstacles to be crossed, to prove the bravery and stamina needed by an "officer" courier's mount. Day three is a stadium jumping test, to assure that the horse, having faced the rigors of day two, is fit and sound enough to continue.

The three-day dressage test is a simplified version of the grand prix dressage, with the same principles and scoring system applied. Three-day stadium jumping follows the guidelines of grand prix jumping, but with smaller obstacles and a less technical course.

The endurance phase, which included a Phase E through the 1956 Olympics, has been shortened to four segments. Phases A and C are roads and tracks, a total of up to 14 miles in length, to be covered at a trot. Phase B is the steeplechase, a 2- to $2^1/_2$- mile course with six to eight steeplechase-type obstacles; the pace is near-racing speed. As soon as the finish line is crossed, phase C begins. There is a mandatory ten-minute hold before phase D at which veterinary delegates check each horse, eliminating any judged not fit enough to continue. Those who pass this check proceed to a $4^1/_2$-mile course spotted with awesomely solid obstacles.

Obstacles on Phase D may include ditches and open water, and jumps up to 3'11" in height and six feet wide at the top of the fence and ten feet wide at the bottom. Jumps are often set into, out of, or right in the middle of water. Also included are banks and drop jumps, which may be six feet on the landing side. Phase E was a grueling one-mile run-in at the speed of 20 miles per hour that has mercifully been dropped. Bonus points, once awarded for bettering the set time for the course, have also been eliminated, and instead penalty points are given for exceeding the time allowed. Courses have become more technical through the years, but jump dimensions remain virtually unchanged from one Olympics to the next.

Organizers have the right to modify distances and speeds in extreme weather conditions, which they have begun to do instead of allowing competitors, like the women previously mentioned, to fall victim to the elements. At the 1996 Olympics in Atlanta, distances and speeds were lessened, and more mandatory holds on course were added to counter the effects of the blazing July heat.

The morning after the endurance test, horses must pass another veterinary exam in order to participate in the stadium jumping. Riders must complete all three days of competition on the same horse for their scores to count. Elimination from one day's test equals an elimination from the entire event. The total score from all three phases is used to determine winners.

★ ★ ★ ★ ★

Army teams were in command of the three-day through the 1948 Olympics in Great Britain. That year the American military team shone in its swan song by winning the gold medal in the three-day, a feat that took their civilian brethren almost thirty years to match. On the other hand, the British military—defeated before a hometown crowd in 1948—was avenged by civilians who claimed their first gold in 1956.

British civilians got a leg up through the foresight and patronage of the Duke of Beaufort. His Grace wrote, "In 1948 the Olympic Games were held here and I had never seen the three-day event competition . . . I went to see our team take part in the cross country which was held at Aldershot and I was very impressed with what I saw, not only by the size of the jumps and the skill of the riders, but also because it was something which could easily be held at Badminton. We have the room to have it, the Park is big enough, and we have the point-to-point course just up at the end of the Park, so there was no reason why it could not be held here. I immediately went to the British Horse Society and asked them if they would back me if I ran it the following April, and held it here in the Park. They agreed to do so and we set to work building the course."

The duke appreciated the display of courage and horsemanship at Aldershot and felt that a properly trained British team could succeed in this sport.

To this end, he not only created a magnificent competition to test riders, but also lent his estate in the early years for team training.

The duke, one of England's most famous masters of foxhounds (his license plate is MFH 1, and he serves as Master of the Horse to the Queen), thought the three-day was a natural for the hard-riding Brits and their bold, fast hunters. Most hunting horses in England are Thoroughbred or near-Thoroughbred and embody the mix of courage, jumping ability, stamina, and speed needed for three-day competition.

Badminton today is considered the best and toughest course in the world—even more difficult than the Olympics. Winning there is the pinnacle of achievement for an event rider, and more than 250,000 spectators flock to Badminton each year to see the spectacle.

Success at Badminton will put any rider from any country at the front of the line when national teams are selected. From the start, British teams were drawn straight off the top of competition at Badminton, unless, of course, the winners were women.

The Badminton Three-Day was first held in April 1949. That year, Vivian Machin-Goodall placed fifth, but for the most part, former military officers dominated. Very soon thereafter, women and foreigners were collecting major prizes. The Europeans had an edge because they were most adept at dressage, and the British women who succeeded did so because they took the time to properly school their horses on the flat. Many of the early converts to the sport were attracted by the speed and thrills of cross-country and considered dressage something to be endured. Their scores, a composite of the total penalties from all three days, suffered from low marks in dressage.

Though women could not ride on the team, they were allowed to serve as grooms, and in such capacity proved invaluable through dedicated and unwavering care for their charges.

One of the girl grooms later wrote about training for the 1952 games, "My fellow girl grooms and I lived in Badminton House under the scrupulous attention of the housekeeper and butler. We had all home comforts and wonderful food . . . Our day began at 5 a.m. and ended at 7 p.m. . . . Great courtesy and consideration was shown by the Duke and Duchess of Beaufort—even to the extent of giving us each a large bar of chocolate for our journey to Helsinki!"

Rules barring women from riding in the Olympic three-day remained in place until 1963, but as early as 1951, women made their mark at Badminton. That year Miss Jane Drummond-Hay (now Whiteley) had a good dressage performance and placed second overall. Since Drummond-Hay was a woman, she was not considered for the 1952 team but was asked to loan her horse First Night to the men on the team.

Women riders who regularly triumphed over men were expected to readily acquiesce to the honor of donating their carefully trained, valuable horses to the team. Margaret Hough lent her horse Bambi V for the 1952 Olympics, though she was not used then due to a rash under her girth, and for Badminton in 1953. In 1954, Hough wrenched her horse away from the all-male team and became the first woman to win Badminton. In recognition of that honor, Bambi V was again commandeered as the reserve team horse for the 1956 British Olympic team. Hough and Diana Mason were invited to ride, rather than simply hand their horses over, in the European Championships in 1954, thus becoming the first British women to tour with their three-day team.

In 1949, Col. W.E. Lyon wrote that to win the gold, ideal owners willing to lend capable horses to the team would have to be found, and that these owners were so rare that "such characters lived vaguely in the regions of that mythical Castle in the Air." That is, unless the owner was a successful woman rider, in which case she was to hand over the reins without a whimper.

In 1956, the twenty-year-old Sheila Willcox, the second-place finisher at Badminton and only 1.5 points away from the win, refused to go along with this, thereby incurring the disapproval of the team organizers and eventing hierarchy. She remembers, "They came to me in the collecting ring at Badminton before show jumping and said they wanted me to make my horse available to the male Olympic riders. I said no. I told them that High and Mighty was my only horse and I had no money to replace him."

The selectors persisted, and the pressure applied to young Willcox was terrific. Finally Willcox agreed to sell, rather than lend, High and Mighty. Ted Marsh, a wealthy sportsman, purchased the horse and lent him to the team.

"Later, the newspapers reported that the horse was lame and wasn't going to the Olympics. I called Ted and asked what was wrong with my horse. He said nothing was wrong. I offered to give him all his money back, and he let me have my horse. He was an understanding and very decent man," Willcox said.

To underscore the fact that there was nothing wrong with her horse, Willcox and High and Mighty immediately began to train for the fall season

Sheila Willcox, shown here on High and Mighty, won Badminton an unprecedented three straight times. Photo: Courtesy of Sheila Willcox.

and were unbeaten for the rest of the year. Willcox won Badminton on High and Mighty in 1957 and 1958. In 1957, High and Mighty won with the best score in the history of Badminton up to that time.

Willcox explained, "High and Mighty was really just an overgrown pony. If you didn't stir him up, which none of the men on the team could do, he'd think, 'Well, too bad, I'm not doing that!'"

In 1958, she unexpectedly retired High and Mighty, who went back to Ted Marsh, a Master of Foxhounds, and enjoyed hunting for a number of years before spending his last days lazing at Willcox's. In 1959, Willcox came back for an unprecedented (before or since) third straight win on Airs and Grace.

Willcox was born a horse lover in a non-horsey family. At age eight, she got her start riding beach ponies at Lytham St. Anne's on England's north shore, where her family had moved to escape the bombing of Britain. Willcox became a handy little helper with the ponies, ferrying them back to their stables at night and sorting out the cantankerous ones.

When she was ten, Sheila coerced her parents into buying her a pony in exchange for going quietly to boarding school. The head waiter at the hotel where she and her family spent the night on the way to convent school said, "Pssst, I have just the pony for you right out back!"

Looking back on the purchase, Willcox said the whole transaction was a joke, since an unbroken two-year-old is the last thing one would select for any inexperienced child. She made a "saddle" from green fabric cut off her father's old billiard table and used knowledge gained through the pony rides, along with everything she learned by watching American cowboy films, to break and train the pony. Her pony Folly proved successful at gymkhanas, showing and jumping, which caused her father to look upon Sheila as "quite a little earner" and to invest in bigger ponies. Willcox competed on them with considerable success in showing and jumping classes until she was seventeen and out of the juvenile classes.

Then, her parents told Sheila she would have to start supporting her horse habit herself. Her first investment was a painfully thin horse that had been used to carry grain for a Yorkshire farmer. She turned the horse, Blithe Spirit, into the National Champion Show Hack and sold him for her first bit of capital. Willcox said, "Luckily, I was always able to see potential in the rough. I had to—that's all I could afford."

Willcox said she possessed a very good eye for stride in show jumping and learned everything she could by careful observation of the best riders. Willcox also learned to turn out her horses to perfection. After conquering the show hack world, in which the best-trained and most handsome horses triumph, she turned her attention to eventing. She worked out her own system of training by logic, as one can witness in her first book, *The Event Horse*. Though written in 1973, Willcox's simple, straightforward, and methodical system could still be used to train a capable horse aimed at the international level. Using her system, Willcox could get one ready in very short order, which brought about her meteoric success.

She found High and Mighty through a *Horse and Hound* advertisement and purchased him for 125 pounds sterling. The pair won a novice event their first time out in 1954. Her rapid rise to the very top of the event world didn't gain her any popularity with the eventing hierarchy. Willcox said, "I had all the wrong credentials. I was of non-horsey extraction, had no money, came from the North, and was also pretty."

Many barriers still existed regarding women riders, and it must have been frustrating for someone so new to the sport to totally dominate. She won Badminton by 80 points.

"I always rode to win. I was never out just for a look at the scenery. If I do something, it's going to be done properly or not at all," she said. This will to win was contrary to the British sense of sports for the sake of sportsmanship alone. Willcox said wistfully, "I think I would have gotten on better in America. I used to daydream about that but never had the money to travel."

Besides her successes at Badminton and at Burghley, England's major fall three-day, Willcox won the individual gold and team gold at the 1956 European championship. She represented Great Britain in the Italian Championships and won the individual gold. In those days international competitions were one year apart, so opportunities to compete abroad were limited. Willcox confirmed that it was immeasurably frustrating not to be able to ride in the Olympics because she was a girl.

It is generally believed that Willcox's many successes, along with the continuing stellar performances of other British women, provided the catalyst for finally getting the rule changed to permit women to ride in the Olympic three-day.

Willcox herself didn't foresee the rule ever changing and retired from eventing in 1961, having settled down to a more staid married life. She said, "The male British selection team weren't in favor of permitting women to ride—they believed women would be too feeble to remount if they had a fall, and secondly, there was the unmentionable possibility of the 'curse' coinciding with a big competition." Willcox never failed to advise one old Lieutenant Colonel—the type who barked—whenever she won while in such a "delicate condition." She said, "I would say, guess what Colonel, I have the curse, and look at me—I'm still standing!"

When the FEI rule was changed in 1963, Willcox scrambled to find a horse with Olympic potential. Glenamoy, a show hunter that caught her eye in a *Horse and Hound* photograph, was purchased after lengthy negotiations. He qualified for Badminton six weeks after the purchase and won Little Badminton in 1964 (by then, two degrees of competition were offered, Little and Great).

As a result, he was placed on the short list for the Tokyo Olympics, with the Burghley Three-Day as the final selection trial. She led after dressage and completed the steeplechase phase with no time faults. During the Roads and Tracks phase leading up to the cross-country, Willcox realized Glenamoy had lost his stamina. During the ten-minute break, she and her team resuscitated him with a well-rehearsed procedure, and it seemed as if all was well. In the cross-country phase, however, he "went" after the second fence. Through sheer determination, Willcox kept him going to the Trout Hatchery with its downward approach to glinting water, dappled trees, and scores of animated spectators. A photograph shows her fall there—both horse and rider are completely under water with just the horse's ears and Willcox's hand, firmly holding her stick and reins, in view. She said, "The faces of the entire crowd show a unanimous transfixion of horror with the exception of one small boy who is howling with delight."

Willcox climbed into her very slippery saddle with one third of the course to go. Glenamoy was restored by his cold shower and finished the rest in better shape than when he started. On the final day, the pair produced "an exemplary clear round."

The selectors, only too pleased not to include a girl, grasped upon the fall at the head of the lake and denied Willcox her spot on the team.

At Tokyo, American Lana du Pont made history in 1964 when she became the first woman to ride in the Olympics. She was also the only woman to ride that year.

Du Pont said, "Sheila Willcox was my hero. She and the other British women were so good, and much more experienced than I was. They should have been first. But I was born lucky, and I was in the right place at the right time with the right horse."

By 1968, Willcox's competition horse, her only one, as usual, was Fair and Square. (Fair and Square was the sire of Lucinda Prior-Palmer Green's Be Fair, the product of a precocious liaison with a mare in the next field when he was two years old.) Willcox called Fair and Square her best horse of all, "He had the lot—tremendous talent, jumping ability, good temperament, and soundness."

Willcox had time to bring Fair and Square the regulation route through summer horse trials, winning most. Then in 1968, Fair and Square won the penultimate selection trial at Eridge over all those on the short list for the Mexico Olympics. At the final selection trial at Burghley, Willcox asked the chairman of the selection committee what it would take to make the Olympic team and was told she had to finish in the top three at Burghley. With her horse properly trained and fighting fit, Fair and Square won Burghley that September in impressive style.

After their win, Willcox joined five riders, including Jane Bullen, who had been training for the Olympics since before Burghley. A few days after her arrival in training, she met Bullen, all dressed up and riding toward the arena. Willcox asked Bullen where she was going and was told that the press was waiting. By the time she had settled Fair and Square and hurried to the arena, the team had been announced, and she was not a member.

Willcox was offered the reserve place on the team. It was made clear to her that her own groom could not accompany the horse to Mexico, and that the horse would be made available to other team members, should any of the nominated horses become lame. Under the circumstances, she turned down the reserve place.

She said of not making the team, "That was really dreadful. I won Burghley and should have been selected. There was an enormous uproar in the press and from the public—it made no difference—but I should have been on that Mexico team with Fair and Square."

In 1971, for the first time in her life, she had two big Thoroughbred-type horses, Here and Now and High and Dry. Willcox felt she had an outstanding chance of finally achieving her ambition of an Olympic gold medal. Both horses possessed the necessary talent, in-depth training, soundness, and trust in their rider.

Willcox placed first and third in the dressage phase of the Tidworth Three-Day in 1971. Willcox remembers her cross-country round on Here and Now, the less experienced of the two, as the best of her life. On High and Dry, a long-striding horse with a very "scopey" jump (great power to take off for a jump from a long spot), she came to a relatively easy parallel bar. Six or seven strides out, she realized the horse would arrive off stride but knew it would be no problem for the talented High and Dry to take off a half stride early. Fate took over. This one time, High and Dry started to take off, changed his mind, set back down, and hit his forearm when he tried to leave the ground too close to the fence. The impact caused the horse and rider to somersault. Willcox, who rarely fell, rode him to the ground, then was catapulted some 20 meters up the field. She remembers waking up and being fascinated by all the blood she saw.

"I tried to get up so I could finish my ride, but couldn't stand. My God, I thought, I'm paralyzed."

She had crushed T-6 and T-7, vertebrae located right about where a bra strap crosses. The vertebrae were crushed, and though the spinal cord wasn't severed, it was badly stretched. After the fall, she was taken to the Tidworth Military Hospital and then transferred to Frenchay, outside of Bristol. She said, "This was fortunate. Had I been in a hospital with other paraplegics, I might have given up, but I was the only one at this hospital. They kept telling me I would never walk again, and I kept saying that I had to walk, that I couldn't afford to be paralyzed."

After five months, she had taught herself to walk again and then how to ride, but upper-level riding was out of the question. Willcox trained and sold horses that went all over the world, and wrote her best-selling book. She starred in a made-for-television movie based on the book. She gave up riding in 1989 when, because of her physical limitations, her riding would have been restricted to "some old dobbins of a horse. The only way I could cope was to make a clean break—eliminating everything horsey from my life.

"In retrospect, I can see that my life was virtually ruined May 20, 1971; although, I did not realize this for many years," she said. Her hopes for the Olympics died that day, and her riding career ended. Willcox said that the constant pain, which has intensified with the years, and the physical limitations and difficulties this has caused, were contributing factors to the ending of close relationships. "There was so much I learned from the experience of being paralyzed for months and having to adapt to a totally new way of life. It taught me a great deal about myself and even more about human nature."

★ ★ ★ ★ ★

The civilian eventing scene in Great Britain began with Badminton—the pinnacle of every event rider's hopes for achievement, then expanded in a downward direction with the formation of lower-level events to provide experience for the up-and-coming. The pattern in the United States started with events on a more provincial scale and didn't work up to international-level competition until Ledyard Farm in 1973. In fact, organizers of early events did not even know what to call their new creations. The earliest efforts were sometimes called "Olympic trials," which they were not, assured Stewart Treviranus.

Treviranus, a Scottish military officer and amateur steeplechase rider, moved to the United States after he rode for Canada in the three-day at the 1952 Olympics. A rider who competed against him in 1954 said he was "the only one of us who had any idea what he was doing." Like Treviranus, others in the United States who excelled in the three-day in the early 1950s came from a military background. Remnants of the U.S. cavalry gallantly brought home a bronze medal from the 1952 Olympics in Helsinki. After that, the next bright spot did not come until the USET's silver at Tokyo in 1964.

The first "Olympic trials" spotted when perusing dusty, long-forgotten issues of the *Chronicle,* were held at the Flintridge Horse Show in California in 1949. The traditional three phases were held on concurrent days of the show. Major George de Roaldes wrote a dressage test for the competition, since none existed in this country at the time. The dressage judges were Hartmann Pauly, who rode on the grand prix dressage team in 1952, and Col. George Huthsteiner. Accompanying photos pictured riders attired for the cross-country phase in smart hunting or horse-show habits, rather than the more informal garb that is favored by riders today. Photos from the cross-country suggest the fences were like those on the outside course used for hunter classes. The total distance of the endurance phase was four miles, of which two miles was roads-and-tracks. The report explained that the goal of the three-day competition was to introduce competitors to the concept, adapting standards to the ability of the riders. Only the jumping phase of the three-day was said to approach Olympic standards. Separate prizes were given for each phase of competition, and women won every one, including the overall competition.

That same year, on the other side of the country, articles in the *Chronicle* announced an "Olympic trials" was to be held at the Devon show grounds in Bryn Mawr, Pennsylvania in September, with the endurance test across Radnor hunt country. Specifications for the competition were widely advertised, but only six competitors entered, all males and former military. The winning mount was Flying Dutchman, the grand prix dressage Olympic mount of Marjorie Haines in 1952; and Hollandia, the mount of William Steinkraus for grand prix jumping at the same Olympics, was second.

Railing against the poor turnout at the otherwise very successful event at Devon, a vexed author penned, "Is it possible that the regular horse show exhibitors are really not interested in advanced horsemanship or is it that they do not feel qualified to undertake tests calling for it?"

One who did care very much about this kind of riding was Gen. Jonathan Burton. Burton was the reserve rider on both the three-day and grand prix jumping squads at the 1948 Olympics, rode on the Joint Occupation grand prix jumping squad that toured Europe in 1949, and was a member of the 1956 Olympic three-day team.

"Wherever Jack Burton was stationed, he would teach international riding to any who wished to learn," said Margaret Warden, who was the initial organizer of the Nashville, Tennessee horse trials, the nation's longest running one-day event.

According to a flyer advertising this event, Burton, stationed at nearby Ft. Knox, Kentucky, on September 1, 1952, "presented the first authentic demonstration of dressage in this section of the country. A group of local equestrians were sufficiently impressed to import the demonstrator, Maj. J.R. Burton, a former Olympic rider, to coach them in this system of riding horse training."

With the help of Burton, Miss Warden staged her first horse trials in 1953. In a flyer for the event, Miss Warden wrote, "As such competitions offer incentive for the continuous improvement of amateur horsemanship and better trained mounts, their adoption in the United States will affect more and better amateur equestrianism. The owner-trainer-rider combination, so neglected, now will come into its own with such tests for well-schooled, versatile horses and riders. If the United States riders are to compete successfully in international equestrian competition, one, two and three-day tests must become widespread in this country."

Miss Warden, a visionary who also founded the first chapter of the United States Pony Club, was over ninety when retelling the story of this competition. She said, "We didn't know what to call it back then, so we called it a one-day." Winners of this first event were Burton and his lifelong friend, Col. Paul Wimert, both of whom continue to serve as combined training judges and technical delegates.

The one-day event was sponsored by the *Nashville Tennessean* newspaper, for which Miss Warden wrote a weekly horse column. The managing editor at the time, Coleman Harwell, egged Miss Warden on to create community horse events that the paper could sponsor. Just one year after her one-day, and again with the support and technical advice of Burton, Miss Warden staged a three-day that really was an Olympic trial. A team was to be selected for the 1955 Pan American Games in Chicago and for the 1956 Olympics.

Miss Warden remembered, "We had a one-day in conjunction with the selection trials. Those with experience said we couldn't do that, but because we didn't know any better, we did."

The facilities at Percy Warner Park, a municipal park in Nashville, were well suited for the event. Already in place were comfortable stables, a steeplechase course, and miles of city-maintained bridle paths, ideal for

Miss Margaret Lindsley Warden chartered the first pony club in the United States and started the first and longest-running horse trials. A hat and white gloves have always been part of her modus operandi. Photo: Courtesy of Jackie Burke.

roads-and-tracks. Rolling terrain and unbroken swaths of well-maintained turf, first carved out of surrounding woodlands by the Works Progress Administration during the Depression, were incorporated into the cross-country.

The event had everything going for it but the weather, and all that those who were involved remember about the event was a succession of 100-degree-plus days, the stifling air of early September, and concrete-hard ground. The temperature was 103° dressage day and set an all-time record of 105° on cross-country day, creating deadly conditions.

In advertising the event, Col. F.W. Boye wrote that the FEI had given its approval for women to ride in all international events, including Olympic dressage and jumping, and was expected to revise its rules on the three-day in time for the 1955 Pan-American games and the 1956 Olympics. A six-member squad was to be selected for training for the Pan-American games.

Two women competed, and one of them survived the cross-country and actually placed. Mrs. William Rochester said, "I don't think they really expected women, but they let us ride."

Elizabeth "Babs" Rochester and her husband lived in Warrenton, Virginia, as did Colonel Boye, so they knew about the event and wanted to see it. They figured if they were going all the way to Nashville, they might as well take horses and compete. It's a little difficult to imagine anyone today who wanted to watch the Rolex Three-Day—the nation's most difficult—deciding to take a horse along to compete, but that was very much the spirit of early eventing in America.

Mrs. Rochester and her husband—described as the real horseman in the family—were hunting folks. To prepare for Nashville, they took dressage lessons from Paul Kendall, a former cavalry officer who was a neighbor of theirs.

Joining in the expedition to Nashville were seventeen-year-old Michael Fields and Joan Harjes, captain of the riding team at the Madeira School, a girls' prep school in Greenway, Virginia with a fine riding program. Bill Rochester drove the van, and the group recruited a white groom, since their regular groom, who was black, wouldn't have been allowed to stay with them in Nashville.

The Virginians arrived in Nashville a week early so they could school over the course. Schooling over a competition course is very much against the rules today, but there really weren't any rules back then, until Stewart Treviranus eventually wrote some guidelines for this new style of competition.

Mrs. Rochester said, "I spent the whole week before the trials leading my horse through the water jumps on the course using an apple as a bribe.

"Before the event started, some retired general lectured the competitors about finishing for the glory of God and country. I raised my hand and asked how fast we actually had to go on the cross-country course.

"That was the wrong question! I was showing the white feather of cowardice," she said. The general made it clear that one was expected to go as fast as possible, "but I was a farm girl. I had seen humans and animals suffer from heat stroke, and I liked my horse too much to risk that. Cross-country day, I had my horse washed down with cold water at every time possible, and I carried ice in my hat. My strategy was to walk in the shade and gallop through the open stretches in the sun. My horse jumped every fence perfectly except one uphill fence, which she ticked."

Mrs. Rochester's horse experienced no difficulty, but half the horses that started the 17½-mile cross-country suffered from heat exhaustion and injuries of other sorts. J.E.B. Wofford collapsed half way around the course on the first of his two horses. Propped up by a local doctor, his parents, and his brothers, he somehow managed to get around the course on Benny Grimes (the mount on which he won the team bronze in the 1952 Olympics) and finished second overall. Frank Duffy won the trials and represented the United States in the Pan American Games in 1955 and the Olympics in 1956. Third- and fourth-placed Jonas Irbinskas was a professional who worked for the Woffords and therefore was not eligible for the team; nor was fifth-placed Michael Fields, who was too young. This left the final berth on the Pan-American team to sixth-placed Walter Staley. Next came Mrs. Rochester. She said, "They weren't interested in me, and I don't blame them. I wasn't very good in dressage and never really got better. The selectors did take notice of my horse, but I didn't want to lend her."

Joining Duffy in the Pan American Games were Wofford and Staley. Staley won the individual gold, but the team did not get three riders around and was thus was eliminated, as it was again in 1956 when Jonathan Burton replaced Wofford on the squad. After the competition was over, Mrs. Rochester, having satisfied her curiosity, returned to her more normal activities of fox hunting and riding in an occasional point-to-point and hunter trials.

Other Virginia fox hunters became interested in the idea of eventing, and those who wished to learn more about it often focused their gaze on Treviranus, who kept his horses in the Blue Ridge Hunt country. In 1956, Blue Ridge started hosting a horse trials, the second oldest American combined training event still in existence. Treviranus was appointed as technical adviser of combined training for the USET and helped teach at a three-week-long event camp, initially held in Woodstock, Vermont. The event camp was later held in various locations around Middleburg, Virginia and evolved into the year-round school that was based at Morven Park, in nearby Leesburg.

Treviranus said that from the first, quite a few women showed up in Vermont to learn about eventing. Of the women at the early clinics, the one who stood out most in his memory was Lana du Pont.

Du Pont was born to a horse-loving family and as a child rode every day after school. Her mother was Mrs. Richard du Pont, breeder and owner of Kelso and many other top racehorses and master of the Vicmead Foxhounds. Du Pont attended her first event at Elkridge-Harford in 1957 when she was a senior at Oldfields, a prep school near Baltimore. She said, "I won. I was the only one to get around the cross-country without going off course."

Donnan Sharp Monk said, "Lana returned home from school that summer and said, 'We really need to learn more about this.'"

Du Pont went to Vermont that year and returned to "learn a little annually" under the tutelage of Gen. Tupper Cole.

In 1960, she started going up to Sunnyfield Farm in New York for lessons from Richard Watjen. Watjen, the dressage coach of the 1948 U.S. dressage team and later of the early civilian British three-day teams, moved to this country to teach grand prix dressage rider Karen McIntosh.

Du Pont said, "We all loved to run and jump, but I needed to learn about dressage. I thought at the very beginning that dressage was critical. It can be taught, and it is a given. You know what is expected. The cross-country is an unknown—you can never know in advance exactly what will be required."

Since the Olympics were closed to women interested in the three-day, du Pont set her sights on Badminton. Her mother gave her Mr. Wister to use on her quest. Du Pont said that riding at Badminton seemed like a far-fetched idea, and initially Mr. Wister seemed an unlikely mount. Her mother said, in a 1962 *The Maryland Horse* interview, "In 1957, I gave up on Mr. Wister [as a racehorse] . . . He was sound enough; his troubles were all in his head. It was simply that nobody could do anything with him."

Mr. Wister was a real rogue with a wicked buck. Du Pont hit the ground almost daily. She said, "I finally learned to stay on him. Once we worked through all of that, he was actually a kind horse."

To further her goal of riding at Badminton, du Pont went to England to study with Capt. Eddy Goldman, following in the footsteps of Michael Page, who won the individual gold for the United States at the Pan-American games in 1959 and 1963 and shared in the team silver in the 1964 and 1968 Olympics. Du Pont's effort resulted in a tenth-place finish in 1961 at

Badminton, the world's most difficult three-day, with what was described as a "workmanlike performance."

This experience gave du Pont a leg up in a sport which was still in a primitive stage in this country. There were not many events, and she once jumped a non-sag farm gate on the Blue Ridge cross-country course because no one had remembered to open it for the competition.

Du Pont and her friend Donnan Sharp organized their own horse trials at Vicmead and somehow even held a three-day, a most complicated task which today would be manned by hundreds of volunteers.

The friends moved from Mrs. du Pont's farm to a cottage at the USET training grounds at Gladstone, New Jersey and drew with them Richard Watjen, who taught them dressage.

As aspiring three-day riders at a time when women still weren't permitted to ride in the Olympics, Donnan said, "I don't really know what we were doing there. I think riders who were serious about improving their skills were welcome at Gladstone back in the early days, and everyone was certainly happy to have Watjen around."

Watjen persuaded Donnan to go for straight dressage—she rode in the 1968 Olympics as Donnan Plumb (married at that time to Olympic three-day rider Michael Plumb), but du Pont stuck with the three-day.

Word came in 1963 that the three-day rules were going to change to permit women to ride, so Donnan, du Pont, and Carol Thompson joined a number of men for a screening trials in Camden, South Carolina.

Michael Page and Michael Plumb, who rode in the 1960 Olympics, were clearly the most experienced and best at the trials. Then came Kevin Freeman, individual silver medalist at the 1963 Pan-American Games. The others sorted themselves out as possible horses fell apart—as a British team selector once said, "Choose your twelve best and by the Games hope that you still have six sound and ready to go." Du Pont was pitted against Billy Haggard, a veteran of the 1959 and 1963 Pan-American Games. Somehow, she secured the spot.

"Billy was the most wonderful sportsman. When Michael Plumb's horse threw a fit on the plane on the way to Tokyo and had to be euthanized while in flight, Billy flew his own horse, Bold Minstrel, over for use of the team," du Pont marveled.

Donnan's horse had accompanied the team as a reserve, but Plumb, then her fiancé refused to ride her horse. Donnan explained that even though she had finished fourth in the National Championship that year, her horse had fallen at every ditch. Plumb had followed along on a motorbike, retrieving the horse for Donnan after each fall. Lana also suffered anxious moments when it looked like she might have to ride Donnan's horse after Mr. Wister came down with shipping fever following his long flight.

"We were located three or four hours from Tokyo. The facilities were first-rate, but the team vet was in Tokyo, and we had trouble getting the support we needed when Mr. Wister was sick," du Pont said.

All du Pont remembers about dressage is watching a few other riders perform and being told by British riders she would be eliminated for being in the arena before her ride. She was frightened to death because she did not realize they were merely teasing the green rider.

Her mistakes on cross-country were caused by a combination of inexperience and shyness. She said, "I didn't have the education or support for the task. If I'd had someone to walk the course with, it would have been helpful. The team coach didn't walk the course with us. I was too embarrassed to ask Mike Page or Plumb about anything. I did ask Kevin Freeman about the parts of the course that worried me most. He was a real friend, and I got through the spots he had helped me with without a problem.

"I got into trouble on the parts of the course I didn't ask about. I had my first fall early in the course. We landed in the middle of a wide jump. We fell because I didn't ride strongly enough to provide my horse with sufficient power to get out of the mud," she said.

Asked what it was like to be the first woman to compete, du Pont said she didn't take much notice but remembers that there were a lot of Japanese photographers running around taking her picture.

Du Pont didn't give up on eventing after the Olympics, but she never had another horse as good as Mr. Wister, either, though she tried a bunch. She married veterinarian W.C. Wright, had kids, became involved with the local pony club, and continued hunting.

Then, about ten years ago, Lana and some friends heard about a combined driving event at Radnor. She said, "Combined driving in those days was in about the same state as eventing had been when I began. My daughter Beale had a Connemara pony, and we had a little cart. Beale might have even driven at Radnor. The event was primitive, but I thought it was some sport."

Her husband gave her a three-year-old, a full brother to Beale's pony, so now she had a pair. Combined driving is a lot like combined training. The dressage, performed in a larger arena to accommodate the carriage, follows the same principles, and in this phase Lana excelled. The marathon, combined driving's answer to endurance, was difficult because the ponies had a hard time matching the speed of the large, strong, European-style horses so often used in driving. Rather than jumps, obstacles include fearsome ditches, steep banks, streams, close-set trees, and fences around which one must wind.

Cones, driving's answer to stadium jumping, were difficult for Lana, but she practiced and practiced and eventually mastered this phase, in which pairs of cones with tennis balls on the top replace jumps. Drivers hasten between the cones, and dislodging a ball constitutes a knockdown.

Soon Lana rose to the top of her new sport, winning the prestigious event at Windsor, England, one of driving's best, for if combined training was Princess Anne's sport, combined driving has been Prince Phillip's since he retired from polo.

This win earned her a spot on the U.S. team in 1989 for the World Championship in Hungary. There, she lost a harness trace during the cones, which is cause for elimination. She got another chance in 1991 for the World Pairs Championship in Austria.

"My only thought was I wanted my score to count towards the team effort," Lana said. She won dressage, finished respectably in the marathon, and went clean in the cones. The U.S. team won their first world driving championship.

Lana du Pont Wright, the first woman to ride in the Olympic three-day, also won the team World Pair Championship in driving competition. Photo: Courtesy of The Chronicle of the Horse.

Now, Lana has taken up yet another sport. In spring 1996, she won her first 100-mile endurance ride. She said, "The pairs are expensive and require a lot of equipment. Pairs also require a lot of help—I couldn't even drive the pair by myself. [Even on a pleasure drive, a groom goes along to open gates, and so on.] I can do the endurance rides myself—all it takes is a horse."

Lana said her own daughter, Beale Wright, is a much more educated rider than she ever was. Beale is a regular winner in horse trials and has had some wonderful horses, but her best have not quite been sound enough to go all the way to the Olympic level. The Wrights have raised some, and Beale's grandmother has given her some, but so far, no luck.

Like the du Pont-Wright contingent, the first woman to represent England in the Olympics was born to the task. There was no question that Jane Bullen would ride, and the probabilities were that she would ride well. She had her first ride at age six months in a special riding basket (an English and Irish contraption used to give children a really early start). Her father was in the cavalry, and her mother raised ponies, a business that's still going strong.

Bullen started showing ponies and moved naturally into eventing through the Pony Club. She won the Pony Club championship, which is a scaled-back three-day.

Her brother, Michael Bullen, rode on the British three-day team in the Rome Olympics in 1960. Her sister Jenny Lorriston-Clark (née Bullen) rode on England's Olympic dressage team.

Bullen chose three-day as her sport, because she said dressage was her sister's thing. In fact, not succeeding in dressage increased the challenge for Bullen and her fleet-footed pony, Our Nobby. Back then, bonus points were given for finishing under the time allowed for the cross-country, so the worse she did in dressage, the faster she figured she would have to go on cross-country in order to offset the bad score.

Bullen was interested in competing in the Olympics but was in nursing school, which made things difficult. In spite of her studies and work shifts, she somehow managed to compete, and in 1967, placed fifth at Badminton and third at Burghley, England's big autumn three-day. In 1968, she won Badminton, though she had pulled night shift before her cross-country. She remembers driving straight from the hospital to the three-day, allowing no time to "get nerved up." That fall she was again third at Burghley.

By that time, riders for the Olympic team were selected on merit—if you were good enough, you were selected; "if you weren't, you weren't," Bullen said. Riders were no longer chosen for extensive training by the team coach. "You had to get there by your own steam. The riders who were picked then trained together for about three weeks."

Five riders trained for the team in 1968. Two were women, and the selectors named Willcox reserve, which meant Bullen would ride in the Olympics. The men who didn't want women to ride in the Olympic three-day in the first place must have been horrified to send a twenty-year-old nursing student on a pony to represent the nation. Bullen said back then, "most men thought women should stay home and warm men's slippers, but the committee knew I was a pretty tough woman, at least equal to the men."

The "old boy" network didn't like taking a woman, but Bullen had the most consistent record leading up to the 1968 games, "even if I was a woman," she said. Then, too, Bullen said, "Our Nobby was an unlikely little chap." Our Nobby measured 14.2 hands at age six, which qualified him for a permanent pony card. Bullen showed him as a pony until competitors complained that he looked mighty tall. Remeasured at age nine, he had grown to 15 hands.

At the Olympics themselves, Bullen and Our Nobby drew attention, he as the smallest horse in the competition, she as a nurse. The press referred to her so often as "Nurse Jane Bullen" that one imagined her riding in a nurse's cape and hat, rather than traditional riding attire.

She rode halfway round the cross-country without any problem, then encountered false ground caused by flooding. Bullen said the longer and further she went, the worse conditions became. Our Nobby couldn't get his feet out of the mud at either of the water jumps late in the course, and after the second fall, Bullen was just hoping to be able to finish.

Her greatest moment of panic was yet to come. When Bullen was standing on the podium to receive her team gold medal from Prince Phillip (who long served as president of the FEI), the men on the team removed their hats. What should she do? Does a woman doff her cap? Does one bow or curtsy when wearing riding clothes? She did not remove her hat, and Prince Phillip almost pulled it off trying to get the gold medal over her head.

Bullen placed eighteenth overall. Our Nobby, age fourteen when he went to the Olympics, was retired after Mexico. Bullen had one more important horse—Warrior—on whom she won Badminton and Burghley in the late 1970s, but she hasn't had anything of Olympic caliber since, and now contents herself with finding young ones, running a training yard with fifty horses, writing books (eighteen to date), and serving on various horse trials, horse selection, and horse society committees. Bullen said, "I've given up nursing, but continue to wake early, and am especially productive between 3 and 5 a.m."

A long list of British women followed Bullen on subsequent Olympic teams. Mary Gordon-Watson won the World Championship in 1970, and Lucinda Prior-Palmer won the European Individual gold in 1975.

Jane Bullen, here with the first-place British team. The American team was second (left to right: Michael Plumb, Kevin Freeman, Jimmy Wofford, and Michael Page), and the Australian team, led by Bill Roycroft (left) was third. Photo: Courtesy of The Chronicle of the Horse.

In America, no woman after Lana du Pont competed for the USET until Jack LeGoff signed on as coach. LeGoff coached the French team and its individual gold medal winner in 1968. LeGoff enjoyed steeplechasing as a youth, won the Championnat National du Cheval de Selle in 1956 and the Championnat de France de Concours Complet in 1963, and rode in the Olympics in 1960 and 1964.

LeGoff was recruited to coach the American team in 1970. He said, "There were only four American riders of international caliber in 1968. One retired, and that was that. There was no coach, no team horses, no upper-level events except for one intermediate event in Virginia, and it had only four starters. We were starting from scratch."

The same year, Neil Ayer took an interest in eventing and signed on as president of the United States Combined Training Association (USCTA). Ayer worked to establish competitions for LeGoff to use as a proving ground for promising horses and riders.

LeGoff held screening trials around the country and constantly attended local events to find the special talent he would need to bring a gold medal

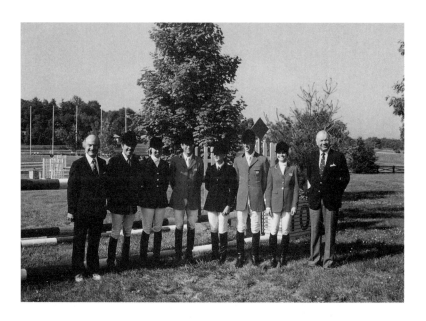

Women got a boost when Jack LeGoff (right) was named coach of the team. He was extremely democratic in his selections. His World Championship squad for 1982 included (left to right) Michael Plumb, Nancy Bliss, Grant Schneiderman, Torrance Watkins, Derek di Grazia, and Kim Walnes. Roland Puton of Rolex, USA, is on the left. Photo: Courtesy of USET.

back to the United States. He would invite thirty or fourty riders for three weeks of training, selecting four or five for more intensive training. Other riders could qualify for consideration at designated selection trials.

LeGoff said, from the beginning, he didn't care about the sex of the rider, boy or girl, "It made no difference as long as they could get the job done."

Before coming to America, LeGoff included the first French woman on a team for Badminton. The British women were beginning to come into their own in the late 1960s and early 1970s, but before that, and after, too, LeGoff said there was definite prejudice against women.

"Everyone has changed a lot. Women were not thought to have the temperament or strength to ride on the three-day team. A man would be taken over a woman of equal or even higher ability," LeGoff said. "There was no reason for that. A journalist once asked me how many woman riders I had training with the team, and I didn't even know. That's how little difference I thought a rider's sex made."

In the first lot of riders selected for intensive training were Caroline Treviranus, daughter of Stewart Treviranus and stepdaughter of Alexander Mackay-Smith, former publisher of *The Chronicle of the Horse* and renowned researcher and author; and Beth Perkins, also from a famous eventing family.

Caroline Treviranus's father had ridden in the 1952 Olympics for Canada, and her mother, Marilyn, did about everything a woman could do eventing from the early 1950s to the 1960s. Treviranus (now Mrs. Leake) said her mother was a rider with great finesse and feel for a horse and that she taught her three daughters well. All three achieved the Pony Club's highest ranking—the "A" level. Treviranus earned her own "A" after she represented the United States in the World Championship—that was how much she and her family valued the Pony Club and its standards. Like many young riders of her era, Treviranus learned a lot about the three-day format while riding in Pony Club, which uses that form of competition for its inter-club rallies.

Treviranus enjoyed success in what events there were back then—she made *Sports Illustrated* in 1963 when, at age 15, she won both the training and preliminary divisions of the local Blue Ridge Horse Trials. Her real rise to stardom came when she met up with Cajun, a just-broken Canadian mare she was asked to ride in a jumper class in 1968. After ten minutes aboard Cajun, Treviranus knew this was the one.

Cajun never even entered the lower-level preliminary competition but went straight to intermediate. Cajun started winning Horse of the Year honors in 1970, and LeGoff put his eye on her. Treviranus said, "Cajun was about 16 hands, with a nice stride. LeGoff invited us to the team and worked our tails off."

As a teacher, LeGoff was much like her mother—Treviranus said. They both stressed using your head and having fun. LeGoff had a great way with a horse, and he taught her and his other riders to listen to the horse—that it is not a machine.

In 1974, LeGoff selected both Treviranus and Perkins to ride as individuals for the World Championship team to compete at Burghley. Four men rode on the team. Bruce Davidson, a LeGoff "talent find," won the individual gold; the experienced Mike Plumb won the silver; and the team, with the aid of Kevin Freeman, won the team gold. Perkins placed sixth.

LeGoff took a quartet of young riders he selected and developed to the Pan-American Games in 1975. Davidson, Perkins, Tad Coffin, and Mary Anne Tauskey, riding in only her second international event, won the team gold.

Tauskey became interested in eventing while her family was living in England. Bruce Davidson remembers meeting her when he was in the process of winning his first World Championship at Burghley. Tauskey tried out Marcus Aurelius at Bathampton House, where Davidson and his bride, the former Carol Hannum, daughter of MFH Nancy Hannum, were spending their honeymoon. Tauskey purchased Marcus, then a novice-level horse (equivalent to the U.S. preliminary level), and brought him back to the United States when her parents returned home.

For Montreal, LeGoff favored younger, though less experienced horses over some older veterans. Tauskey was named the lead-off rider for the team. Davidson remembers that she was tough, hard-working, and determined. Marcus, only 15.1 and slightly built, was known as the "Bionic Pony."

Tauskey's success put Treviranus No. 6 when the lineup for the Montreal Olympics was named. Treviranus said, "As No. 6, I might as well have been No. 206. I wasn't going to ride."

In spite of her own disappointment, somewhat lessened by the fact that her horse Comic Relief was USCTA Horse of the Year, Treviranus doesn't know how the team selection could have been done any better. She praises the work LeGoff did with the team and the fairness with which he treated selections. Unlike acrimony felt by riders on some other teams, LeGoff had a knack for keeping unity and harmony throughout—no matter how competitive his riders were, they were friends through it all and out for the team results.

In 1976, just six years after the "LeGoff" method was put into effect, the United States won its first Olympic three-day gold since the days of the army teams. In 1972, LeGoff had used his only three riders with previous Olympic experience along with Bruce Davidson, then a fledgling, to win a silver. In 1976, he used Plumb and Davidson again, with Tad Coffin, who won the individual gold, and Tauskey, the first woman to represent the United States on the three-day team since 1964.

Tauskey became the first American woman to win a team three-day gold, and her victory was followed in quick succession by two American women who helped earn the team gold at the 1984 Olympics in Los Angeles.

There, Torrance Watkins, who then rode as Torrance Fleischmann, and Karen Stives climbed the podium beside Davidson and Plumb. Stives won the individual silver and very nearly the gold. Four years earlier, Watkins had won the individual bronze at the Alternative Olympics, held in Fontainebleu. Jimmy Wofford won the individual silver at Fontainebleu, but the American team was eliminated because the other two riders failed to complete. At Fontainebleu, additional individuals were allowed to compete, and Stives, not a member of the team, placed thirty-fourth overall.

LeGoff retired in 1984, and America did not win another medal until 1996, though the team has not failed to include a woman for this most

Karen Stives, shown here with The Saint, won the team gold and individual silver at Los Angeles. She is now the popular head of the team selection committee. Photo: Courtesy of USET.

demanding sport. In 1988, the team selection was based on placings in designated trials. That year, Phyllis Dawson, Karen Lende (also a member of the 1996 team, riding as Mrs. David O'Connor) and Ann Hardaway Taylor (who rode as Ann Sutton) joined Bruce Davidson. Dawson was the highest placed of the American riders, and perennially successful Virginia Leng took home the individual bronze and team silver for Great Britain. At Barcelona in 1992, Jil Walton, a newcomer to the upper echelons of eventing, was the highest placed on the American team. Another newcomer, Jill Henneberg, got her chance at Atlanta as part of the silver medal–winning team.

Women have already accounted for every major eventing honor except the individual gold medal. LeGoff, who has been in position to watch eventing for a long time, has no doubt that a woman could, given the luck needed, win the individual three-day gold medal.

Women's Race Track Suffrage, or "This Isn't Going to Be a Problem"

KATHY KUSNER HAS SUCCEEDED AT ANY NUMBER of objectives the less bold wouldn't have considered. She said, "There have been times I've been told 'You can't possibly do that.' Then I figure, I want to do that, and I'm not doing it now, so what have I got to lose by trying?"

Her quest to obtain a license to ride at pari-mutuel race tracks was certain to be successful, but Kusner hated to be the first woman to make the attempt.

As early as 1964, friend and fellow steeplechase rider Dr. Joe Rogers told Kusner that because of changes in the law, she would be able to get her race rider's license if she tried.

"I kept thinking one of the race track girls would file the suit," Kusner said. "I had another life, too. I was also involved in show jumping, and the USET. Applying for a professional jockey's license was going to take a lot of time and commitment."

Kusner rode anything and everything—not only hunters and jumpers, but also racehorses. "I would ride in any race of any flavor," she said. She had ridden in pony races, and by sixteen (the youngest age permitted), was riding in ladies' timber races at the Virginia point-to-points.

Kusner said, "In one pony race we drew for mounts. I tried to bribe the child who had drawn the best-looking pony a dollar to switch mounts. She wouldn't, so I flailed away at my shaggy beast and won anyway."

Some bush league race meets had no rules, period. Women were permitted to ride; in fact, Kusner said a space alien could have ridden. There were no regulations, and little sobriety. Culpeper, Virginia, had such a meet. They had two races—one per day. At one such meet, Kusner won both. This was race riding at its toughest. Fights and shenanigans were the norm.

Other more staid opportunities for women to ride included Pimlico's Ladies' Race, begun in 1937 as part of the build-up to the Preakness. The contestants in this race did not swing broken bottles at one another, but neither were they bound by certain standard racing rules, such as crossing the scales. Women (blush, blush) wouldn't want their weight revealed (and still don't, when it can be avoided).

Race meets occasionally carded sprints for Quarter Horses, and Kusner once rode the same horse to win two of these sprints in one day (a joint venture with fellow Olympian Frank Chapot). She said, "We won the daily double with a single entry."

After graduating from high school, she galloped horses for Maryland-based trainer D.M. "Mikey" Smithwick. Smithwick, one of the few steeplechase riders in the Racing Hall of Fame, trained horses for Mrs. Theodora Randolph. Mrs. Randolph, her long-time supporter, felt it was good for Kusner to spend some time around Smithwick, a well-regarded racehorse trainer and an all-round horseman.

As much as Kusner enjoyed racing, her international jumping career with the USET took most of her time, but she tried to always spend August at Saratoga, New York. For that month each summer, the best trainers, horses, and riders in the world gather at the hallowed spa, and Kusner reveled in the race track life. At daybreak, Kusner would work horses on the track with the likes of racing great Angel Cordero, Jr. then school steeplechasers in the infield. In the afternoon, she would watch the races and yearn to ride. Trainers would tell her, "Too bad you don't have a jock's license, we would give you some mounts."

Kusner observed, "Of course they would say that—they had nothing to lose. I couldn't get a license."

Kusner thought about riding races as she drove back from New York to Maryland the summer of 1967. By the time she arrived home, she thought, "I'm twenty-eight years old. I've got to try to get my license. If I don't try now, it will be too late."

Audrey Melbourne, with Sister Siglinde Hartmann, used knowledge of the riding and legal system to win a landmark case for women. Photo: Courtesy of Judge Audrey Melbourne.

"I asked the starter at the track if he would take a look at an applicant for a jockey's license. He said certainly he would. The night before Kathy was to ride, I called a friend on a newspaper and said, 'Would you like to see history made?'"

Life at a race track begins before dawn. Horses have to be exercised and off the track by 10 a.m. so the track can be worked before the afternoon races.

That particular morning, clusters of reporters and TV cameras formed in the predawn gloom. Melbourne knew the starter she had selected loved an audience. If he was surprised to see a woman ride out of his gate, he was effusive when the cameras were rolling and microphones were thrust under his chin. How did she do? Oh, fine, fine, "good enough to ride anywhere, as good as I've seen," the starter poured forth as long as he had an audience to listen.

One down, two to go. Mikey Smithwick was only too happy to sponsor Kusner. She would still have to prove to the stewards at the track that her riding was up to par, but it was time for her to hand in her application to the Maryland Racing Commission.

Kusner said, "I got to the racing commissioner's office, and the TV cameras were there too, thanks to Audrey. The commissioner would not even touch my application. I was walking forward while the commissioner was walking backward. I was holding the application out to him, and he had both hands behind his back. The cameras were whirring. Finally, I placed the application on his desk. That night, the film footage was all over the evening news.

"I don't like publicity. It is an interruption to your life. It robs time that could be used more effectively and interestingly for other things," Kusner said.

However, in this case, because the story was so widely played, she got a break. Melbourne said, "I got a call from the Marjorie Cook Foundation, offering to underwrite all legal expenses and to aid Kusner in starting her racing career."

Mrs. Cook's father, a wealthy Baltimore judge, left half of his estate to her brother outright but put her half in a trust to be managed by her brother, "because a woman obviously wouldn't be capable of handling her own affairs," Melbourne said. "Well, Mrs. Cook was so insulted by her treatment that she left her entire estate to aid the legal status of women. Trustees of the foundation read about Kusner's case and came to us and offered to help."

Kusner's case exemplified the spirit of the Marjorie Cook Trust. The trust was flexible enough to even provide Kusner with a two-pound saddle, which enhanced the tools needed for her career as a jockey. But first things first. An angel had been found for what was to become a protracted legal fight, in spite of Melbourne's initial optimistic predictions. It was to take one frustrating year for the case to reach fruition.

The stewards were the first major obstacle Kusner and Melbourne faced. Just getting three of them gathered to watch Kusner ride was a trick. Melbourne said, "You've never heard such excuses: [It was] too foggy. They couldn't spot her in a group of horses. Can't be there that morning, and on and on. Eventually they watched Kusner and said that, no, she didn't ride well.

"We appealed the stewards' decision to the Racing Commission. Everyone was lined up, including the press. The stewards said she wasn't good enough. We showed films of her riding in the Ladies' Race at Pimlico, a Maryland track. Her performance did not suggest that her skills were inadequate."

"Next, the starter took the stand. He testified, no, Kusner should not be approved. We started the tapes rolling again—this time with the starter's enthusiastic endorsement for the TV cameras," Melbourne said.

Mikey Smithwick said flatly that Kusner was more than good enough to have her license, that the commission denied her simply because she was a woman.

The Maryland Racing Commission changed its stance. Maybe Kusner was capable, but they would have to turn her down because they lacked adequate changing facilities for women. No problem, Kusner said, she would not mind changing in the ladies' rest room. Well, then, the commission countered, they were turning her down to protect the two-dollar bettor. Bettors surely would not back a woman, and that would upset the odds. (Odds for a race are set by the bettors themselves; the horse that commands the largest bet proportionally is assigned the shortest return on the tote board, should he win.) She couldn't possibly be granted a license—she was an amateur. Kusner assured the commission she had made arrangements with the USET to stay within the letter of the Olympic law, and her business dealings weren't any of their concern, anyway. Melbourne thoughtfully reminded the board that Rigan McKinney, a wealthy amateur sportsman, had achieved such a record in steeplechases at the Maryland tracks that he was inducted into the Racing Hall of Fame.

Kusner's longtime jumping teammate, William Steinkraus, said with admiration, "The Racing Commission spent hours talking down to Kusner and Melbourne as if they didn't know anything. The men patiently explained all the reasons a woman could not possibly be a licensed jockey. Melbourne listened politely through all this insulting rhetoric, then took them off at their knees."

The Jockey's Guild also threatened to be troublesome in the process, but Melbourne summarily dismissed them with an antitrust lawsuit claiming unfair labor practices.

Undaunted by logic, reason, good judgment, or a sense of fair play, the racing commission turned Kusner down in three separate hearings. *The Blood-Horse,* Thoroughbred racing's most respected trade journal, editorialized in its December 9, 1967, issue against the unfairness and lack of logic displayed by the racing commission.

When all legal avenues had been exhausted within the Maryland Racing Commission, Melbourne was free to take her case to the state court. She presented the case to the state attorney general's office. "Don't know when we can get around to reading this," she was told. Melbourne responded, "Don't worry—we'll wait!"

Melbourne wanted to have the case heard in Prince Georges County, where she was most familiar with the system, and got Kusner to live there for the duration of the proceedings. (Years later, Melbourne became the first woman elected to circuit court there. She currently serves as judge of Maryland's Seventh Judicial District.)

"I thought all along that we would be able to get the license through Maryland's administrative law amendment, so I pushed the case into circuit court. According to this law, the case couldn't be pursued any higher, but I thought I could do a lot under that law."

"You're asking an administrative body, in this case the Racing Commission, to give you a license to do whatever. If you can show you're just like everybody else in the same position, but that the administrative body acted differently in your case for no valid reason, it's an administrative law case.

"The Maryland Court determined that the Racing Commission had acted in a capricious, arbitrary, and discriminatory manner based solely on the sex of the applicant," Judge Melbourne explained.

After the frustrating months with the Racing Commission, Kusner said, "To say the circuit court decided the case in thirty seconds would be an exaggeration. It was more like nine seconds."

Since that decision was handed down, all capable women in America have been afforded the same opportunity as men to obtain a jockey's license. Other schemes were used to prevent women from riding in pari-mutuel races, but no racing commissions in other states followed the example of the Maryland commission.

Kusner said, "What was always so frustrating was I was being denied an opportunity solely because I was a woman. I know men who were granted their license promptly, though they had no riding background. One worked in a Laundromat and was told, because of his small stature, 'You oughtta be a jockey.' He got his license, but I couldn't, though I had devoted my life to being a rider."

In October of 1968, *The Blood-Horse* was still editorializing against the pig-headedness of the Maryland Racing Commission. In November of the same year, that magazine, along with other trade journals and newspapers around the world, chronicled the landmark decision to grant a woman a jock's license. The outcome of Kusner's case was reported as far away as South Africa.

If the case drew plenty of publicity, it earned Melbourne some snide remarks, as well. She remembered hearing sports reporters, seated near her in court, commenting that if she didn't have anything better to do with her time than to try to get a woman a jockey's license, perhaps she could try to get Shirley Temple onto front line of the Green Bay Packers.

Because of this case, Melbourne counseled in other similar cases. She was called for advice when Barbara Jo Rubin became the first woman to apply for her license in Florida, and helped a neighbor, Mary Ryan, fight a suspension issued by the National Steeplechase Association (NSA, formerly the NSHA).

Riders' licenses for the flat tracks are approved by each state's racing commission, a state-appointed board. Steeplechase licenses are issued by the NSA and its elected board. The NSA is a national organization incorporated in the State of New York, so Melbourne contacted an attorney licensed in New York to represent Ryan. She briefed the attorney on the case against Ryan, and he was eager to present her case to the NSA. Melbourne, the New York attorney, and Ryan took their complaint to the National Steeplechase Association in Saratoga (the organization's base during the month of August) with all guns loaded.

Melbourne chuckled, "We walked into their office to argue the case; they looked at us and said they would be delighted to remove the suspension against Ryan."

Ryan (Mrs. Joe Hirsch), who now works for the New York Racing Association, had been issued a $10 fine for a minor infraction but along with it, an indefinite period of suspension. She said, "They didn't want a girl to ride at Saratoga."

An official of the NSA at that time later admitted the board was not all that delighted to have women riding. The official said though women had been doing fine in powder-puff derbies and in ladies' point-to-points, it was feared "they would lack the strength to race against men."

On remembering her most famous case as a lawyer, Melbourne said, "Many believe Kathy's case was argued under some equal rights provision, but I did it the old-fashioned way—the way I had been taught in law school. Nothing flashy, just solid groundwork."

★ ★ ★ ★ ★

Mary Ryan got to ride at Saratoga with Audrey Melbourne's aid. Photo: Courtesy of Mary Ryan Hirsch.

Jane Thorne Sloan won many steeplechases in England and the United States. She said facilities for women in the U.S. were way behind those provided in England. Photo: Jackie Burke.

If all aspiring women jockeys in America benefitted from the efforts of Melbourne and Kusner, women riding in England did not. The English women riders had many opportunities to obtain race riding experience at the numerous point-to-points in that horse-loving country. There, however, it did take an equal-rights amendment to clear the way for women to obtain riders' licenses from the Jockey Club, England's national governing board.

In England, the Sex Discrimination Act was passed December 29, 1975. In January 1976, women began knocking at the door of 42 Portman Square, the Jockey Club headquarters. Because of the newly passed law, the Jockey Club was required to issue riders' permits to either sex on equal terms. The terms were: (1) Stewards must be satisfied of the applicant's competence, and (2) Applicants must be recommended by licensed trainers.

The first woman to apply was Mrs. Sue Horton. She had won her first point-to-point at age fourteen and had been five times national ladies' point-to-point champion. She had won forty flat races and six hurdle races in Europe. It took eight and one-half minutes for the Jockey Club to agree to grant Mrs. Horton her license, which was done on the 27th of January, 1976.

Muriel Naughton was the first English Jockey Club–licensed woman to ride. She did so on January 30, 1976, beating only one horse in an amateur steeplechase at Ayr, Scotland. After that, women began riding on a regular basis.

It was the Thorne twins, Diana and Jane, who came first to the winner's circle. Diana, an accomplished event rider and now wife of successful National Hunt trainer Nicky Henderson, beat her twin to the punch. Diana and her father, John Thorne, finished one-two in the first hunter chase of the season, February 7, 1976. Two weeks later, Jane, now married to amateur steeplechase champion George Sloan, became the second English woman to win under the National Hunt rules of the Jockey Club.

Winning the Race Against the Male Establishment, or What Part Don't You Understand?

KATHY KUSNER'S COURT CASE WAS THE FIRST CAMPAIGN IN THE WAR to get women jockeys onto the race track. After her case was settled by the Maryland Circuit Court in November 1968, the battle began in earnest.

With the ink fresh on her Maryland jockey's license, Kusner planned to start her new racing career as soon as the fall indoor show circuit ended. Instead, she broke her leg while riding for the USET at Madison Square Garden and hobbled into winter on crutches.

Kusner did not regret missing the honor of being the first woman to ride as a licensed jockey. She said, "Thank goodness I wasn't the first. The publicity was intense the first year. Publicity is very disruptive. I just wanted to quietly ride like everybody else."

Quietly, like men could, that is. Life was anything but quiet for the first women jockeys.

Penny Ann Early could have been the first to ride. She was the first to apply for and receive her license in Kentucky. On November 19, 1968, she was the first woman to be named on the "overnights" to ride at a state-licensed track. (Overnights are entries for an upcoming day of races,

Women rely on a partnership with their horse, rather than brute strength, to win races. Jane Sloan accounted for many wins aboard Spartan River. Photo: Pat Casey Daley, The Nashville Tennessean.

although horses listed don't necessarily start in the race. The trainer may decide the competition is too tough. The horse may not be "right" due to a training injury or not being in peak condition. The race might overfill, in which case, a blind draw is held.)

In Early's case, she was replaced by the horse's regular rider, who had become available. This is not unusual, as there is a pecking order for first call by trainers and for certain horses, and the best jockeys are often overbooked.

Three days later, on November 22, Early was once again named on the overnight for Churchill Downs. This time, she was still listed to ride the horse on race day. The press box that day was reminiscent of Derby week, with a mob of out-of-town reporters on hand to see history made.

Early was dressed in her silks and ready to go, but her race was postponed. The male jockeys staged a boycott, the first in Churchill's ninety-four year history. Early's race was switched from the fourth to the ninth and last race on the card. The stewards worked feverishly to persuade male jockeys to ride against Early. Two-and-one-half hours later, the boycott was ended when Early was replaced by a male rider.

The New York Times referred to Early as "the country's shapeliest jockey." Other publications described Early as an "attractive blonde." Reporters wrote that she had been assigned to ride at 113, but weighed 117 pounds, and she had therefore avoided the embarrassment of being the first overweight woman jockey. Kathy Kusner hadn't missed a thing by sitting out this dance.

Woman who were ground-breakers could not have thin skin. Penny Ann Early was tough and lived a hard life, according to Tom Proctor, whose father, Willard Proctor, employed her as an exercise rider for about twenty years. Her flashy style—the shortest possible mini-skirts, long hair, and plenty of makeup—invited the comments bantered about in the papers. Whenever Early had a public appearance, the senior Proctor, a no-nonsense, plain-spoken trainer of the old school, used to tell Penny Ann, "For goodness sakes, wear a --- ---- dress!"

Willard Proctor, now based at Santa Anita, said not every male jockey objected to riding against Early. Some of the best didn't mind a bit, but other riders came to Proctor and said, "You sure dirtied up the dishes by having a woman work for you." Proctor mentioned to the objectors that they hadn't been too proud to accept rides from lady owners or trainers.

When Early came to work for Proctor in 1965, women were still a rarity on the "backside." In 1954, *Sports Illustrated* listed Mrs. Joan O'Shea in its "Milestones" column, as "one of the few women exercise riders in America."

Tom Proctor first saw women on the backside in the mid-1950s. They rode lead ponies, the well-broken mounts used to escort high-strung

Thoroughbreds to the track. Next, women were hired as hot walkers. Proctor, who now trains horses himself, said Early was a good gallop girl and he'd
love to have riders of her caliber in his barn. He currently employs a woman
as his "bug," or apprentice jockey. (Apprentices receive a significant weight
allowance in races, thus providing trainers with incentive to give them a
chance. With slight variations from state to state, a jockey loses this weight
advantage one year after winning three races.)

Willard Proctor's training operation, like many racing stables, functioned
as one big family. Penny Ann often slept on the Proctors' couch and carted
young Tom and his brothers around with her. On one memorable evening,
she took the boys to see *The Graduate*. What Penny Ann saw on the screen
embarrassed her, and she tried in vain to get the youngsters out of the
theater.

Today the movie would probably rate PG-13, but back then, the com-
edy about a college graduate and a sophisticated older woman was a shocker.
Tom Proctor said, "The world [in the late 1960s] was changing so much—
the Beatles, Kent State, and student protests."

An editorial in *The Blood-Horse,* May 3, 1969, began "Rebellion is in the
air. On the streets, and college campuses. In ghettos and courtrooms and
committee meetings. At the race track."

After the jockey boycott, Early went to Mexico to ride in a match race at
Caliente and vowed to stay on the West Coast and get her jockey's license
there.

The Churchill season was over. Most of the trainers who had been in
Kentucky loaded up and shipped to Florida. It was here that the next battle
was fought, led by Barbara Jo Rubin and Bryan Webb.

Barbara Jo Rubin had begun her quest to become a jockey after graduating from high school in Florida. A local trainer had been coerced by his
biggest owner, who was Rubin's uncle, into taking her into his barn at Tropical Park. (Tropical Park has since been replaced by the Calder track.) She
worked for the trainer for free and, in return, was allowed to ride one horse
per day on the track.

A few female hot walkers worked at Tropical Park at that time, but they
were not universally welcomed. Rubin said some trainers would not let her
so much as set foot under their shed row on her way to the track kitchen.
Women were banned from the backside altogether after 5 p.m. This meant a
woman trainer couldn't even come back to the barn to check water buckets
at night.

When the stable that employed Rubin moved to New England for the
summer of 1968, she went too. Since she wasn't being paid, Rubin, who

could no longer count on meals at home, got hungry. She started galloping for other trainers. Many of them wanted to hire her full time. She would ask each trainer if he would give her a chance to ride in races. The trainers scoffed at such a suggestion. Kusner had not yet won her case in court. Neither Rubin nor any other woman held a jockey's license. Even so, Rubin remained steadfast in her belief she would be able to ride. She said, "I knew I was good, and I knew things were moving on. Times were changing."

Finally, trainer Bryan Webb, who did things differently than most trainers anyway, said he would let Rubin race his horses if she could get her license. So she signed on.

An article about Webb, entitled "Woes and Girl Riders," appeared in the November 30, 1968, issue of *The Blood-Horse.* Webb's stable had been winning but was wiped out in a barn fire at Suffolk Downs in May 1968. When the *Blood-Horse* article was published, Webb's stable consisted only of empty halters, but he was going to Florida to get them filled. Webb joked, "Buying horses is easy. Paying for them is the tough part."

Having Rubin, a woman with aspirations to become a jockey, in the barn wasn't helping his chances to rebound. Webb defended Rubin in the article. "She's good, and she's strong. I'll ride her [in races] as soon as she can get a license."

The article concluded, "A fellow trainer retorted in disgust, 'Nuts. Put her in a tight spot, and watch her take up [get frightened and slow down her horse].'"

In December 1968, after Kathy Kusner and Penny Ann Early had been granted licenses in Maryland and Kentucky, respectively, Rubin applied for her apprentice license at Tropical Park.

The stewards there didn't know what to do with the application. Rubin filed for a hearing with the Florida State Racing Commission. The Civil Liberties Union was geared up to carry her fight onward if necessary, but the State Racing Commission didn't need to be hit over the head with a placard. On January 10, 1969, at their regular monthly meeting, the commission amended Florida Racing Rules to permit female jockeys to compete in races against males. In compliance with federal anti-discrimination laws, the rules were changed, and in any spot where the word "masculine" appeared, "feminine" was added. Tropical Park was instructed to give Rubin a fair trial. On January 13, 1969, Rubin passed her schooling test for the license "with something to spare," according to the reports.

Rubin was scheduled to ride in a race at Tropical Park on January 15, 1969. The crowds were immense. Reporters from all over the nation came to cover the event. Rubin sat huddled in a makeshift changing room in the

Red Cross trailer. A brick was hurled through the window at her as the tension-filled afternoon ticked away.

Anticipating trouble, Webb named her to ride in the last race of the last day of the race meet. If other riders boycotted it, the plan was for Rubin to mount up, ride to the post, and walk across the finish line, and thus be declared victor in a walkover. The record-setting crowd would have its show, and the trainer and rider would have a win.

This wouldn't be the first win Rubin had achieved through guile. As a teenager, she often participated in unsanctioned races held on abandoned airstrips and other clandestine spots where men met to gamble and prove whose horse was the fastest. (These were just like the drag races teenage boys used to hold on deserted roads.) Because Rubin weighed less than the other riders and rode better, her mounts usually won. The money was usually bet against "the girl," so her backers were rewarded with long odds.

Rubin started riding through an unlucky, lucky occurrence. At age six, before the Salk vaccine had been invented, she contracted polio, the dreaded crippler of children.

Rubin's doctors prescribed swimming as physical therapy to stretch out the disease-weakened muscles and ligaments behind her knees and her painfully drawn lower legs. This didn't work. She could not move her lower limbs sufficiently to keep afloat. She remembers wearing iron shoes to help anchor her feet to the ground and having her feet tied to the wall when she went to bed at night in a vain attempt to keep her legs straight. Then a doctor recommended riding, which she thought was a splendid idea.

Riding helped to strengthen her lower legs and ignite a love of horses that continues to burn to this day. Her parents, not horsemen themselves, were understandably grateful for their daughter's progress and were ready to support her riding interest in any way possible. Rubin took lessons and learned to ride all kinds of horses.

She was not to ride that day at Tropical Park, though. The "mighty little men," as publications described them, started a boycott during the fifth race, causing chaos in the packed clubhouse. Again, the stewards quieted restive crowds by replacing the woman jockey with a man.

The Florida Racing Commission demonstrated they would not tolerate such behavior. Protesting riders were fined $100 each. Word went out that the next such display would result in a fine of $200—maybe as much as $500. Jockey's Guild representatives advised jockeys not to accept mounts if they were not prepared to ride against women. There would be no defending protestors in the future, and punishments would escalate if men again resorted to a boycott.

A disappointed Rubin went to Nassau in The Bahamas to ride in races. The rest of the traveling circus of trainers and riders moved on to other Florida tracks.

"The excuses were so lame," Diane Crump remembered. "The jockeys would say they wouldn't ride against a woman because of 'the riders who had died for the sport.' What's the point of this? It clearly wasn't a woman's fault that those men had been killed on the race track!"

Diane Crump could have been named to ride at Churchill. She was there at the same time as Penny Ann Early. Trainer Don Divine (later her husband and father of her daughter, Della) was ready and willing to name Crump to ride in a race, and his biggest owners wanted Crump to ride, too. However, these owners also owned the Churchill race track and wanted someone besides Crump to test the waters, because they were anticipating trouble, which came when Penny Ann Early attempted to ride. (In 1970, track owner W. Lyons Brown underscored his belief in Crump's riding ability when she rode his horse in the Kentucky Derby, the first woman to do so.)

When Crump moved to Florida with the Divine string, Mary Keim, a trainer who was pushing for the rights of women riders, kept naming Crump on the overnights, but her mounts didn't draw in to the over-filled races.

Crump was galloping a horse at Gulfstream, readying for the soon-to-open meet there, when she heard from other riders that she had been named on the overnights for the next day's racing at Hialeah, another Florida track about thirty minutes away. She didn't even know the trainer who submitted her name.

Crump had to borrow racing tack and was forced to change clothes in the Horsemen's Benevolent Protective Association (HBPA) office. Armed guards escorted her to the paddock and physically protected her from the crush of the crowd. The number of spectators at Hialeah on February 7, 1969, matched a record set when Swaps ran there after winning the 1955 Kentucky Derby.

George Johnson, Jr., a supervisor of the Florida State Racing Commission, was quoted as saying, "If they [the male jockeys] back out now, God help them. They had their chance to take off at scratch time. They better not try anything at the last minute."

But the men had finally gotten the message that the Florida Racing Commission was playing hardball. The back of the protest was broken. The jockeys mounted their horses for the seventh race, and it was business as usual.

Diane Crump was Tampa's "official yearling breaker" when she was still in high school.
Photo: Courtesy of Diane Crump.

What was it like riding into the starting gate under the intense scrutiny of the world? Crump said all she could think was, "Finally—at last."

The papers agreed that her mount, Bridle 'N Bit, was in over his head. Not unexpectedly, he could do no better than 10th in the field of 12, but none found anything to criticize about Crump's ride, a ride she'd been preparing for since she started skipping school to work with horses.

Growing up, Crump had always wanted a horse. Her parents lived in suburbia on Long Island. Her father promised that some day they would move to Florida and he would buy her a horse. The family moved when Diane was thirteen, and her father made good on his word.

Then, Crump needed an income to support her horse habit. She got a job handling Lake Magdalene Farm's weanlings (foals just taken from their mothers). When the weanlings became yearlings, the lightweight and eager Crump was asked to break them.

There were only four Thoroughbred farms in the Tampa area back then, and there was a lack of qualified horsemen when the local race track was closed. Crump became the local yearling breaker.

When the youngsters she had broken for Lake Magdalene went to Sunshine Park (now Tampa Bay Downs), Crump went with them. She got to walk hots and jog horses in the shed row. Soon, she was riding on the race track.

Less than a month after her historic first race, Diane Crump won with Tou Ritzi at Gulfstream Park. Crump gave up race riding in 1984 so her daughter, Della Divine, could enjoy a more normal life. Photo: Courtesy of Diane Crump.

When Sunshine Park was open, she skipped school to be at the track. The stewards constantly tossed the underaged Crump out, but she would climb over the fence or be spirited in by trainers who would hide her in the back of their cars. She finished her senior year of high school in March, ahead of her class and at only age sixteen, by attending night school.

At age sixteen, she was off to the races. Crump headed to Gulfstream, then to Pimlico in Maryland with the Lake Magdalene string. Her parents let her go. In the first place, they couldn't stop her, and in the second place, the farm's owners were a close-knit Italian family who treated Diane like one of their own five kids.

When the Lake Magdalene horses returned to Florida, Crump stayed at the track. She moved from place to place, galloping for some of the leading trainers.

Unlike Rubin, Crump never had a notion that she might be able to ride in races. Crump said, "I never thought about it. Society was so ingrained in its position toward women, you just couldn't imagine what you could do.

"Then I heard about Kathy Kusner's court case and thought, all right, yes, we can do it. I want to [ride in races] right now!

"I was prepared for the task. I had learned everything from the ground up. I progressed naturally from the weanlings to the yearlings to two-year-olds. I was ready to work for trainers by the time I was a senior in high school. I weighed 110 pounds and was strong and fit. It's not a matter of strength anyway, but how you get along with the horse."

Kusner's court case had let the genie out of the bottle. There was no going back to being content with simply galloping horses. Crump wanted to be a jockey.

After her record-breaking ride at Hialeah, she went to ride at her hometown track, Sunshine Park (Tampa Bay Downs). The attitude there surprised and stung her. Rather than being welcomed as a returning hero, she was shunned and condemned for "stepping out of line. Those people knew me best. They knew how hard I had worked to get this chance, but they couldn't change their thinking," Crump said. "I thought, don't we have the right to do what we have in our heart to do? Why are we not equal?"

In racing, the naysayers predicted that women jockeys would cause accidents on the track. The percentage of injuries to men did not rise, but women, once they got into the game, had numerous opportunities to be injured themselves.

Barbara Jo Rubin rode and won in Nassau on January 28, 1969. She then rejoined Bryan Webb's stable, which had moved on to Maryland. A short while after her return to the States, she got angry with Webb and went to Hot Springs, Arkansas to be with her boyfriend. She stayed in Arkansas only three days.

Rubin said, "My boyfriend was a jockey. His friends assumed I'd given up my dreams of racing. They told him to marry me and get me pregnant so I'd forget about riding. I went straight back to Maryland and made up with Bryan."

Webb named Rubin to ride in a race at Charles Town, West Virginia, February 22, 1969. She changed clothes in the First Aid trailer. Guards had to keep back crowds who were tearing at her, trying to get scraps of her clothing as souvenirs. Even with all the distractions, Rubin was not bothered. The race was at night, and she had been awake since before dawn to work horses. It was cold, and if anything, she was sleepy.

Rubin mounted a colt named Cohesion. She broke from the gate on top, laid third or fourth for most of the race, and rode her horse out to win.

How did it feel to be the first woman in America to win a race? Rubin said, "I was doing my job—period."

The media universally described her as shy and modest. Rubin simply didn't think working hard and doing one's best was much to crow about. She is not slow to share the stories of her early racing career, and speaks with plenty of enthusiasm when describing her life today at the Great Southern Mule Connection, a horse and mule farm near the Okeechobee Swamp. Like Kusner, she just wanted to quietly do her job and go about her business.

Rubin said the track management at Charles Town was great, and most of the riders were okay, too. Not all the jockeys welcomed her, though, and she had to run the gauntlet to prove her worth. Some male jockeys would deliberately push her wide or would whip her in the face with a

Barbara Jo Rubin became part of the traveling show of women jockeys so in demand once women started racing. Rubin, upper left, is pictured at Sunland Park in New Mexico, 1970. Patty Barton, lower left, was one of the most successful women jockeys until a severe head injury ended her career. Her daughter, Donna Barton, is a leading woman jockey in the 1990s. Photo: Courtesy of Tom Dawson.

"misdirected blow aimed at their own mount." When stewards would ask her what had happened over on the far side of the track, Rubin never ratted on them. Eventually the riders started respecting her.

Rubin won nine of her first eleven starts. Then things started going wrong for her. She, like the other women jockeys who quickly followed suit, became part of a traveling sideshow. Tracks wanted woman jockeys because they drew large crowds and massive amounts of publicity. Powder Puff Derbies, once scheduled for fun and contested by amateurs, were major features, easily filled with the growing number of women who rode as licensed professionals. Rubin was constantly traveling. She found it difficult to diet and to maintain a reasonable exercise program to keep her weight down. Instead of riding horses she knew, she had to race anything that came along, and some of them were bad. She started having serious falls. No sooner than she would recover from one bad injury than she would have another serious spill. Eventually, she gave up her racing career. She worked as an assistant trainer, then a trainer, and now has a multifaceted horse operation. She specializes in driving but dabbles in other aspects of riding, as well.

Diane Crump continued race riding until 1984, when she decided to settle down to one spot so her daughter could lead a more normal life. She took over the training barn at the fabled Calumet Farm in Lexington, Kentucky. When that job ended in 1987, Crump moved to Front Royal, Virginia, near her parents and so Della's high school years would not be disrupted.

Today, Crump walks with a limp and wears a knee brace, as witness to permanent injuries caused by falls. Yet, she is tan, fit, and otherwise healthy and, at forty-six, still youthful in appearance. She exercises the horses she trains in the mornings, and in 1996, twenty-five years after her first race, she rode two of her charges to wins at Laurel in Maryland.

When the horse bug bites, it seldom lets go. Julie Krone, the most successful female jockey in the world, can't imagine a life without horses. Krone, too, has overcome life-threatening injuries to continue her career but hasn't given any thought to when, or why, she might retire.

Krone said she sometimes suspects there might be other interesting aspects of life going on outside of her universe but that she hasn't yet considered giving up the physical discipline and constant danger of being a jockey to seek them out.

"I'm never a normal person. I live, eat, and breathe horses. This addiction helps you," Krone said.

Krone, whose normal weight is 100 pounds, follows a strict diet to keep her energy level high. She forgoes the pleasures of going out to dinner, or any other late-night entertainment that would compromise her form as a world-class athlete.

The list of records Krone has broken as a woman jockey goes on and on. She was the first woman to win a Triple Crown race—the Belmont aboard Colonial Affair. She has been the top money-winning rider at Gulfstream, Belmont, Monmouth, and the Meadowlands. She has won five races in one day at Monmouth and was the first rider to win six races in one day at the Meadowlands.

"This is the life of my dreams. I love my job. In the mornings when I'm on the track, getting along with the horses I'm riding, I think 'This is so beautiful. I'm so lucky,'" Krone said.

Even when she's not at the track, she's riding. One of the fruits of her financial success—mounts she has ridden have won more than $50 million—is that Krone can now keep her own riding horse at a "full-service" boarding barn. When her morning workouts at the track end early, she calls the barn and tells them what time to have her horse ready. She then gets into her car, picks up coffee at a take-out restaurant, and makes the leisurely 15-mile drive from Belmont to Old Westbury.

"My horse is as fat and slick as a wet seal. The farm is beautifully run. It has an all-weather riding ring, a good set of jumps, an indoor ring, and perfectly manicured trails over 2,200 acres. My horse is blooming mentally from the care he is receiving," Krone said.

Things have not always been this plushy, but Krone's life has always revolved around horses. Julie's mother thought it was good for children to have animals and to have free range of the out-of-doors.

Her father is a professional photographer, so Julie's life with horses has been well documented. In an early photograph, Julie's first pony, Dixie, gazes lovingly at his five-year-old rider, as she enthusiastically grasps her first riding trophy. The next pony in the family album is an exquisitely formed, but "diabolical" pony named Filly. Julie's jaw is set, and she is devoting her full attention to Filly.

Krone said that part of her desire to become a jockey began when she read *The Kid,* the story of *Wunderkind* Steve Cauthen, the youngest rider to win the Triple Crown. After reading about the riding successes Cauthen accumulated by age seventeen, she knew what she wanted to do with her life. She shared her dream with her mother and also with famous dressage instructor Chuck Grant. Grant, rather than laughing at the precocious Miss Krone, told her gravely that if she wanted to be a jockey she should read everything she could about racing, then try to get a job as a hot walker.

Julie and her mother studied every book and article about racing they could find. Julie's parents were divorced, and Julie and her mother lived a very frugal existence. Mother and daughter worked in a local riding barn, and at night, her mother waited tables in a bar. All of her tips went into a glass jar to save up enough money to visit Churchill Downs during spring break from school. The Krones left for Churchill Downs with enough money to buy gas and to stay for three days. Fortunately, her mother quickly found a job as a hot walker. Trainers were not so eager to hire the child-sized Julie, but by the end of the day, she had talked Clarence Picou, a young trainer, into letting her work for him. Julie said neither she nor her mother knew any better than to wear high-heeled cowboy boots to work that first day, and they paid for their mistake with blisters that lasted for weeks.

Julie and her mother returned to Michigan after the spring holidays were over, but Julie went back to Kentucky to work for Picou that summer. She stayed with the trainer and his wife, Donna.

Julie wrote in her autobiography, *Riding for My Life,* "The night before my mother drove me back to Churchill Downs to spend the summer . . . we saddled our horses and went for a ride. It was past midnight and the moon was almost full, shining silver on the road as we cantered along. We sang the song "Don't Fence Me In" at the top of our voices. . . . It was not the last time we would ride together, but it was the last ride we took as mother and child."

Julie wrote of her intense loneliness that summer. Even though the separation was keenly felt, she did not give up on her dream of becoming a jockey. The next summer, her mother arranged for Julie to work for a friend whose husband trained Quarter Horses in Michigan. Julie would get an opportunity to ride, and to race on the Midwest Fair circuit.

Julie returned to school that year flushed with the success of wins at the Quarter Horse tracks. School had always been a miserable experience for Julie. Years later, her academic problems could be attributed to dyslexia, a disturbance in the perception of letters of the alphabet, coupled with Attention Deficit Disorder. Back then, students so afflicted were accused of being disruptive, slow, or lazy. Rather than prolong this kind of torture, Julie's mother permitted her to drop out of school at Christmas of her senior year, go live with her grandparents in Florida, and work at Tampa Bay Downs.

Lacking proper credentials, Krone and her mother followed the path used years before by Diane Crump and climbed over the back fence. With her win pictures from Michigan in hand and bravado that towered above her 4-foot 10-inch frame, Krone talked trainer Jerry Pace into giving her a chance. Within five days, she had been granted both an exercise license and an apprentice jockey's license. Her mother returned to Michigan, satisfied that Julie was well on her way to realizing her dream.

When the Tampa Downs meet was over, Krone went to Maryland. Chick Lang, Jr., a jockey's agent, took her on and treated her like one of the family, literally. Krone moved in with Lang, his wife, and their four children.

Krone pushed and pulled and wheedled rides. Eventually, she lost her "bug" and became a journeyman. Trainers use apprentices when they want to get their horses a weight advantage. Riders who have never won any race are assigned 10 pounds less than journeymen, 7 pounds after the first win, 5 after the third, and after the fifth, 3 pounds remain off for the rest of their apprentice year. To even out differences in their ability, horses carry specially designed weights. One pound equals a one-length advantage in a mile race, so trainers use apprentices when they need a tactical advantage. Once a rider becomes a journeyman, he has to be able to ride 10 lengths better than a beginning apprentice. Krone said not every rider achieves this degree of proficiency, and some careers end when the bug runs out.

A case in point is Kathy Kusner, who started all of this for women when Julie was riding her first ponies.

"My career, if you can call it that, was severely compromised by the fact that I never had a bug," Kusner said. Due to a peculiarity in the apprentice rules, riders over twenty-five may not ride as apprentices.

"Trainers had no incentive to give a totally inexperienced jockey a ride."

But Kusner did get a chance when Billy Christmas, a trainer with a string in Pennsylvania, called out of the blue and asked her to ride for him. She rode a total of over 400 races in her career as a jockey. Like the other early women jockeys, Kusner said she was often on tour and chalked up many of her wins in foreign countries.

The elegant, sophisticated Bert de Nemethy, Kusner's coach on the USET, initially decried her jockey career. Yet his enthusiasm eventually rose to the degree that he acted as her agent, procuring a mount for her at Baden Baden, the stylish spa in Germany. None of her teammates could go—just Kathy and Bert—and their efforts resulted in a smiling win picture in which de Nemethy holds Kusner's horse while she receives her trophy.

Great things did not follow, Kusner said. "I had two strikes against me. I never had a bug, and I was a woman."

Krone's career did survive the first of the two challenges Kusner mentioned. She won her first race at Atlantic City as a journeyman and got a really big break when John Forbes signed her on as a stable jockey. This was a big stepping stone. Krone said that every jockey wants to be associated

Kathy Kusner rode a number of winners for trainer Billy Christmas (left). Here she set a track record at Marlboro, Maryland, on Terrible Tiger. Photo: Courtesy of Kathy Kusner.

with a stable, and to be a rider for a string the quality of Forbes's was "major." Hustling as a prevailing life form could be left behind. She could now set about riding for and learning from Forbes.

Krone said she could not remember at what point trainers stopped looking at her as a girl who wanted to be a jockey, and started looking at her as a professional rider. Maybe her parents could pinpoint a date, but it had been so long since she had thought in those terms, she herself could not say.

"Now I can look on my career as a natural progression. First, I rode at Tampa Downs. I didn't know anything then. When I came to Maryland, I was still very inexperienced. So, did trainers not want to give me a chance because I was so inexperienced or because I was a girl?"

Krone got a wake-up call on the rights of women when she rode in Japan four or five years ago, however.

"Racing in Japan is huge," Krone said. "Three times as many people as can fit in the Giants' stadium come to the races. They bet $1.7 million on a maiden race."

Bets of $350 million are placed in the Japan Cup, the nation's biggest race. Krone was suitably impressed by all of this but was buzzing around riding races, business as usual. After winning a race, the reporters asked her what it had been like to be the first? First what, she asked, first woman to win that race? No, the first woman to race in Japan, she was told.

"I wanted to say, 'Get out of here. What are you talking about?'" Krone said.

"In spring of 1996, I read that the first four women jockeys had just graduated from Japan's Jockey School. That's major. I like to think my riding there might have helped change those women's lives."

Kusner's court case certainly changed things for all women who wanted to be jockeys in America, if not so much for Kusner herself. She said that riding no more races than she did, she never got as fit as she needed to be. Though Kusner, who runs in ultra-marathons, would work up to eighteen horses in the mornings, she didn't get enough of what one can only get by riding in races.

Krone agreed that there is no substitute for riding in races. She said, "You can work and work and work a horse in the mornings as fast as you can, but still become exhausted in a race. After I had been riding in races regularly for about six months, I remember thinking, 'I'm finally fit enough to do this.'"

"Race riding is a combination of aerobics and yoga and gymnastics. You have to master all aspects in order to be successful," Krone explained.

Comparison tests with other professional athletes show jockeys to be the fittest of all, and riders like Krone prove women, given an opportunity, can achieve a winning level of mental and physical fitness.

10

Steeplechasing—You'd Never Hear a Girl Say That

IN 1971, KATHY KUSNER WAS OUT IN FRONT, poised to strike another first for womankind. In 1964, with commitment, talent and hard work, she was one of the first two American women to be included on an Olympic jumping team. In November 1968, with patience, perseverance, and years of experience learning the trade, she was the first woman to be awarded a professional jockey's license. When she was named to ride in the 1971 Maryland Hunt Cup and the race committee appeared ready to bar her entry, the wishing and hoping stages were over. Kusner burned with sheer determination.

"I had been riding in point-to-points since I was sixteen. I had been riding races on the flat. I could jump," said Kusner, who already had two Olympic games to her credit.

Kusner's ability to ride over the solid timber fences of the Maryland Hunt Cup course could not be doubted, though the unadorned verticals, some of which stand 5'3" in height, make it the most difficult jumping course in the world. To prepare for her ride, she had walked the course with D.M. "Mikey" Smithwick, who had won six Hunt Cups, and had gotten a lot of advice as to how to ride the race. Smithwick had also given her mount's owner/trainer, Kris Lindley, the benefit of his knowledge in preparing Whackerjack for the task.

Kathy Kusner, aboard Whackerjack, was the first woman to ride in the Maryland Hunt Cup. Photo: Douglas Lees.

The committee balked because Kusner was a woman. John Rossell, in his excellent *The Maryland Hunt Cup, Past and Present,* wrote that her entry had been "the big talk before the race [and afterward] . . . No lady had ever been so nominated before, and though the conditions did not say so specifically . . . it had always been understood that the Hunt Cup was for male riders."

Kusner said the Maryland Hunt Cup committee held an emergency meeting the night before the race to decide what to do about her entry. Turney McKnight, an attorney and an active rider at the time, advised the committee that the jig was up. They could not deny Kusner an opportunity to ride. She had already beaten the Maryland Racing Commission in the Maryland courts when she got her jockey's license, and there would be no defending their actions if they refused to allow her to ride.

Kusner still feared there might be trouble at the Hunt Cup on April 24, 1971. "The first woman to enter the Boston Marathon had been grabbed out of the race. One thing I could envision was someone pulling my horse's bridle off and chasing him away, leaving me standing there with no horse," Kusner said.

No such incident occurred. Rossell wrote that the 1971 Hunt Cup must be put down as one of the best fields since its inception in 1894. Twelve horses started, including three previous winners. All the winners finished ahead of her. Four horses fell. Kusner survived the towering timber fences to finish sixth. She had done as well as her mount, Whackerjack, could be expected to do.

Two years before she rode in the Hunt Cup, Kusner received her amateur rider's license from the National Steeplechase Association. (The NSA formerly granted two tiers of licenses—amateur and professional.) Races sanctioned by the NSA are generally referred to as "steeplechases," and differ from point-to-points in that money purses are offered, and depending on a state's racing rules, pari-mutuel wagering may be allowed. Riders in NSA events must either be licensed or receive special permission to ride in that day's events.

On April 12, 1969, three women requested and were granted permission to ride in the Middleburg, Virginia Spring Steeplechase. Kusner's case against the Maryland Racing Commission made it clear that women would have to be permitted to ride, sooner or later. The race committee, rather than risk a lengthy and expensive court case, accepted the women's entries.

The women who were nominated, Katherine "Kassie" Kingsley (née Chatfield-Taylor), Ready Snodgrass, and Mary "Mikey" Ryan (now Mrs. Joe Hirsch), were well known to the committee and just as important, to the male riders. None of the male jockeys raised any protest.

All three slated to ride at Middleburg, like Kusner, had considerable experience on the Virginia point-to-point circuit. Virginia, with its many point-to-points, was a very good place for new riders (even women!) to start. Mrs. Nancy Hannum remembers riding in cross-country races for foxhunters in Virginia when she was a teenager in the late 1920s and early 1930s. The Warrenton Hunt started its cross-country race, open to hunting men and women, in 1934. Other hunts quickly followed suit. By 1936, these cross-country races were evolving into the modern point-to-points, which are very much like sanctioned steeplechases. Mrs. Hannum said that from the start, point-to-points in Virginia, Maryland, and the Delaware Valley always included a ladies' race on the program. Though women were restricted to the ladies' timber race and an occasional flat race, there were numerous races of this sort in which women could gain experience. The ladies' races had, and still have, large entries and keen competition.

Kingsley moved to Loudoun County, Virginia, the birthplace of her mother and grandmother and great-grandfather, at age seven, and was given her first pony, a nice Shetland bred from her great-grandfather's stock. By age nine, Kassie was hunting and showing ponies of good quality for neighbors. The Loudoun Pony Club was founded, and Kingsley rode on its winning "C" team in the area's first regional Pony Club rally. Radio star and dressage rider Arthur Godfrey, who lived in nearby Waterford, lent the Loudoun team his van so they could go to the first national Pony Club rally, which was held in Nashville, Tennessee. Kingsley, age thirteen, won the written test, had the best dressage, and went clean in both stadium and cross-country. She was awarded her "B" Pony Club rank on the spot.

From age thirteen Kingsley then went to convent school and rode only in summer, hunting over school holidays. Rather than attending college, she made her debut in Baltimore and worked with polo ponies. Kingsley still has fleeting visions of careening out of control over the top of a hill and toward a wire fence on a crazed polo pony. She retired from that line of work and, though only seventeen, was hired as riding instructor at Garrison Forrest, a private girls' school in Baltimore. During this period, she hunted with Green Spring Valley and worked in the mornings for Mikey Smithwick, who has developed so many good race riders. She rode in pairs races with Harry Wight, joint master of the Loudoun Hunt, and he asked if she'd like to ride in a ladies' race.

"I rode at the Piedmont Races. My mount, a whipper-in's horse, was content to go on top. I was so far ahead that I let my horse ease as we neared home, and Sally Strawbridge came past me from way back. I had to scrub like a washerwoman for second place. The owner couldn't have been nicer—he was so pleased with his horse's performance. I would have taken me off the horse and never let me ride again," Kingsley said.

Kingsley did get to ride again, though. She was champion lady rider of the Virginia circuit in 1968 and 1969. One of her regular mounts in 1969 was Lenoso, a bit of a rogue that had not proven a suitable mount for owner Archibald Kingsley. Kassie was asked to ride Lenoso in the sanctioned meet at Middleburg, if they could get permission for her to do so.

Kingsley had already ridden the course at Glenwood Park, used for the sanctioned meet, in the Middleburg Hunt Point-to-Point. She said it was

Kassie Kingsley and Lenoso won often in the Virginia point-to-points. Photo: Douglas Lees.

very exciting to be permitted to ride in the Middleburg Hunt Cup at the sanctioned meet. She said she made some amateurish mistakes in her race and finished in the middle of the pack.

Kassie married Lenoso's owner that summer, and for their honeymoon, the couple went to England to ride in point-to-points. She continued to ride in point-to-points when the couple returned home to Middleburg but quit after receiving a bad bump on the head in a schooling accident. By then, she was mother of two little boys, and six months after her fall, she was still having trouble remembering simple things like their names. The little boys for whom Kingsley abandoned her own racing career are now both winning races themselves. Her son Arch was third on the leading riders' list after just three years, and her son George won the first sanctioned steeplechase he entered. Kingsley boasts that she is a "top producer" and said that trainers come to her and ask if she has any more sons at home.

Ready Snodgrass came to Virginia by way of numerous other ports of call. Her father was career Navy, and the family followed him around the world. At age five, Ready talked her non-horsey family into breakfast rides at the local dude ranch in Kansas. She learned hunt seat in California and western riding in Hawaii. Eventually the family came to Virginia, where she further developed her jumping skills. She read an old book entitled *The Horsemasters* and dialed a phone number listed for the British Horse Society's riding certification program. Because of this serendipitous call, Snodgrass found herself at Porlock Vale Riding School in England, where she earned her assistant instructor's license. When she came back to the States, she went to work for Harry Wight and became interested in hunting and point-to-points. She got her first ride in the Casanova Point-to-Point in 1967.

Casanova, first race of the season, is infamous for its weather, and that year it was 16 degrees with a 40-mile-per-hour wind. Snodgrass was second of two and had a wonderful time. She started working for Tom Beach, an excellent horseman who loved the point-to-points. She helped Beach in Casanova each morning, then drove 70 miles to the other side of Leesburg to Wight's in the afternoons. In between, she rode for Bonnie Bell at Tomwood Farm (now Interhorse) in Middleburg. She was the first woman hired to break the fabulous yearlings at Paul Mellon's Rokeby Farm. She kept a few of her own horses on the side. Her mother kept asking when she was going to get a real job. Snodgrass said, "I never had any money, but I loved life and rode a lot of horses."

Snodgrass had ridden a hurdle horse at Oatlands, one of the few point-to-points in which women could jump other than timber, and the trainer asked if she would ride the horse at the Middleburg Steeplechase. She said, "I grinned all over, said yes, then was scared to death."

There was a lot of discussion, but she, Kingsley, and Mary Ryan did get to ride. She said, "I finished back in the crowd. I thought, I really did it. I didn't do anything too stupid."

Snodgrass applied for her NSA rider's license that day. She and Mary Ryan were both granted their professional jockeys' licenses. Snodgrass's rides in sanctioned races were few and far between. She finally won a sanctioned race in the early 1980s. She didn't travel, so her sanctioned rides were limited to the Middleburg meet. In 1982, she rode in the Virginia Gold Cup. Snodgrass is pretty sure she was the first woman to ride in the Gold Cup; she finished fourth, and is almost certain she was the first pregnant woman to ride in the Gold Cup. In 1983, local point-to-point champion Patti Cassell rode in the

Gold Cup, and Jane Thorne Sloan finished second aboard Spartan River, a horse bred in England at her father's stud farm.

After Snodgrass's daughter was born, she didn't race again until she started riding her marvelous horse, Tom's War, in the 1990s. She took the ride on Tom because she felt other jockeys weren't doing the horse justice.

With his owner aboard, Tom's War won three races in 1992, was Virginia Steeplechase Association's Timber Horse of the Year, and voted to the same honor by the point-to-point association. That year, Snodgrass misjudged the final fence at the Old Dominion Point-to-Point and took a bad fall, thus missing the lady rider honors, which she did win in 1993 for the second time in her life, having first won in 1967. Of the horse sports, she said steeplechasing best soothes her "adrenaline addiction" and is about the best hobby a body can have.

Mary Ryan, who apprenticed under champion jockey Joe Aitcheson's father, rode in the most races of any other woman that first year. She had ten

Mary Ryan rode That's Me (number 6) to second place at Fair Hill shortly after she became one of the first women to get her professional rider's license. Photo: Courtesy of Mary Ryan Hirsch.

races to her credit when she fell in a race and was badly injured by oncoming horses.

Vivian Rall was the only woman to win a race that year. She won a turf race at the Far Hills, New Jersey meet on October 25, 1969, aboard her own horse, Father's Footsteps.

In his year-end review, NSA executive secretary Cooper wrote that 1969 "saw the breaking down of a custom as old as racing itself. Both in steeplechasing and in flat racing, female riders competed against the male sex on equal terms." He observed that the women were more carefully scrutinized than novice male riders would have been and outlined some of their rookie mistakes. However, he admitted that "at times they had shown a fair degree of ability."

Women continued to ride in steeplechases when they could get a mount. Snodgrass, Rall, Ryan, and Kusner were joined by Jennifer Youngman, Joan Boyce, Joey Ruhsam Reuter, Toinette Phillips (now Mrs. Louis Neilsen), and Elizabeth Zemp.

It was not until the Radnor, Pennsylvania meet on May 17, 1975, that Barbara Kraeling (now Mrs. Richard McWade) became the first woman to win a sanctioned steeplechase over fences. According to the account in *Steeplechasing in America,* Joey Ruhsam also won a flat race that day "to add further affront to the male ego."

Kraeling's non-riding parents permitted her and her sister to take lessons at the local riding academy, hoping this would "cure" the horse thing. By age twelve, both girls were working students for horseman Johnny Beach (huntsman for the Harts Run Hunt, and uncle of Thomas Beach). They stayed in the barn all day whenever they could, and showed and hunted, as well. At age fourteen, Barbara went to Virginia with Beach and rode in a few point-to-points. She was too young, but since she was "real tall," officials thought she was sixteen.

The only time Kraeling remembers getting in trouble for breaking the rules was when she planned to cut class to go hunting. This would be easy since she drove her own car, but she couldn't figure out how to get her hunting clothes past her parents, who were watching TV in the den. Kraeling decided to drop them out her second-story window, but her mother looked out just in time to see the rain of riding clothes.

Her parents either never learned about or never acknowledged another of her little peccadillos. She bought a horse without their knowledge and took it with her to college at Penn State. The horse was boarded on a little farm near the campus, and on weekends in spring, she would ship the horse down to Tommy Beach's and go to the point-to-points with him and his daughter, Virginia Beach, who was a leading woman rider.

For her last two years of college, Kraeling transferred to Seaton Hill College in Greensburg, Pennsylvania, just 15 miles from Ligonier and the legendary Rolling Rock Club. Back then, Rolling Rock hosted a terrific two-day steeplechase meeting, fox hunting, and a summer show circuit. For those two years, through a lucky break—the man who held the job had broken his leg—Kraeling was hired to show horses for the late Gen. R.K. Mellon. She lived in the barn apartment over his exquisite English-style stable, with its richly paneled trophy room and sunny courtyard.

After teaching school for a few years, Kraeling got another lucky break, again literally, and was hired to fill in for the injured whipper-in of the Rolling Rock Hunt. During this time, she raced her own horse, Fuzz Ears, under the tutelage of huntsman and excellent horseman Lovell Stickley.

Barbara Kraeling and Fuzz Ears beat the boys at Radnor. Photo: Courtesy of Barbara Kraeling McWade.

When Barbara broke the ice at Radnor, she had already ridden Fuzz Ears (whose dam, or mother, was Smart Hussy) in a number of amateur races at the sanctioned steeplechases and had been riding for years in point-to-points. She said there was no difference between riding in steeplechases and in point-to-points, but it was nice to win a purse.

Fuzz Ears was injured the following year, and though he could be hunted after that, Kraeling had no more racing stock, so her steeplechasing days were through. Joey Ruhsam and Toinette Phillips Neilson rode for outside owners against the pros, but Kraeling just raced her own horse. She said, "If you were an amateur like me, you had to have your own horse or an 'in.' No one would have hired me to ride."

Kraeling moved to Middleburg to work as an assistant to Rick Watters, son of trainer Sidney Watters. She eventually started training on her own, married jockey Richard McWade, bought a place, and had a baby.

"My father had no interest in horses and criticized my efforts. After he died, I was touched to find he had collected the steeplechase yearbooks [which have articles about the races and complete charts of every race]. He had underlined everything in those books that was written about me," she said.

Even though Joy Slater Carrier had an "in" that Barbara and any other aspiring steeplechase rider would envy, she also had to wait to ride in steeplechases. Both her grandmother, Mrs. Miles Valentine, and her mother, Jill Fanning (formerly Slater), owned large racing stables. Mrs. Fanning, former MFH of the Essex Fox Hounds, also trained her own horses.

Carrier, born at a time when she might have gone straight into open competition, was restricted to riding in ladies' races at the point-to-points. She said, "If I had been a boy, I would have started riding in steeplechases at age sixteen. Instead, I rode in horse shows.

"Mother was once asked by the NSA to join the board of stewards. She declined because she said women should not serve in that position," Carrier explained.

It was not that the women in her family were shy. Carrier's great-grandmother arrived by boat from England with her three-year-old daughter in her arms, but without her husband by her side. She settled in Philadelphia and opened the London Flower Shop. Carrier said, grinning, "Back in my great-grandmother's day, women didn't do things like that. I come from a strong female line."

Carrier has a photograph of her great-grandmother, grandmother, and mother riding sidesaddle together. Joy, too young to be riding on her own, is being carried in front of her mother. Soon enough, Carrier was able to take her place in the line, riding sidesaddle in the family class at Devon each year with her mother and grandmother.

Joy was a member of the Essex Pony Club and hunted during holidays from boarding school at Foxcroft. Her horse showing was limited to summers because her family believed school came first. Starting in June 1971, she managed to scramble around and qualify for both the AHSA Medal and the ASPCA Maclay finals. Frank Chapot, who was busy showing in the international classes for the USET at the Pennsylvania National Horse Show and awaiting the birth of his first child, found enough time to polish up Joy to win the AHSA Medal finals.

Her parents pushed academics through high school, but when it came to college, Joy was free to make her own decision. She chose to study advanced horsemanship with Iris Kellett in Ireland.

While studying with Miss Kellett, Joy rode as the sole member of the American team in the Royal Dublin Society Horse Show CSIO. Due to an epidemic in the United States, Ireland closed its borders to American horses but permitted Joy to show, since she was already there.

After Joy returned home, she rode in ladies' races. May 5, 1976, she finally got to ride "under rules" in a sanctioned steeplechase at Fair Hill, Maryland. There were four girls in the race, and they finished first, second, fourth, and fifth in a full field. Joy won aboard her mother's horse, Moe Green. Joy had already won a ladies' timber race on the horse, but when a male rider tried to race him, Moe flipped in the paddock. This gave Joy her chance. She won, then won again the next time she rode him, beating another good horse of her mother's that finished second.

Joy said, "I rode the horse; he won. A boy rode; he flipped. I rode, and he won, then won again. What does that tell you?"

It told her mother and other owners maybe Joy could come out of the ladies' division.

Her grandmother purchased Cancottage, a good English horse that owner Broderick Munro-Wilson had imported to ride in the 1979 Maryland Hunt Cup. Mrs. Fanning trained the horse, and Joy was given the ride for the 1980 Hunt Cup.

The conquering hero that year was Charles Fenwick, Jr., who had just won the English Grand National and was home in time to begin a sweep of the Maryland timber races with Dosdi, the winningest timber horse ever. Their streak came to an end just shy of the Hunt Cup when Dosdi was injured, and Fenwick was suddenly without a mount. The Hunt Cup was thrown wide open.

Accounts of the race call it one of the most thrilling in history, with Cancottage and Beech Prince hooking up for a fierce duel over the final three fences to the wire. At the finish, it was Joy and Cancottage.

Joy Slater teamed up with her grandmother, Mrs. Miles Valentine (left), and her mother, Mrs. Jill Fanning (right), to win the Maryland Hunt Cup in 1981. Photo: Douglas Lees.

The victory came as a complete surprise to Joy, who hadn't planned to stay for the annual ball. She had to borrow a dress from a friend so she could accept her honors. That night, Jay Meister, one of her friends and a fellow timber rider, was dancing with an older lady, who asked him what he thought of women riding in the Hunt Cup. Jay responded that if the woman were qualified and had the horse for it, he thought it was all right. The woman said, "You've had too much to drink, young man," and left him standing alone in the middle of the dance floor.

Such an attitude did not discourage others from following Kusner and Carrier. Carrier (riding under her maiden name both times) won again in 1981. Turney McKnight's wife, Elizabeth, won in 1986 (Turney won in 1982).

Sanna Neilson won in 1991 and 1993. (Neilson's father, Louis "Paddy" Neilson, has won three times, and her uncle, Charles Fenwick Jr., six times. Her aunt Anne Fenwick trained the winner in 1993. Sanna's ancestors on her mother's side first won in 1898 and again in 1904.) In 1991, Sanna became the first woman to win the Virginia Gold Cup.

Sanna Neilson, aboard Joe's OK, trained by Alicia Murphy, was the first woman to win the Virginia Gold Cup, beating her uncle, Charlie Fenwick (middle), on Ivory Poacher, the horse Nielson rode to a victory in the Maryland Hunt Cup, and Gerry Newman (right). Photo: Douglas Lees.

Joy took her chances in the Grand National in 1984, after several seasons of riding races in Ireland. She and her husband, Rusty Carrier, spent time there after their marriage, and Rusty's horse, King Spruce, won the 1981 Irish Grand National with Gerry Newman aboard (Gerry's wife is successful professional show horse trainer and rider Kathy Doyle Newman).

Starting in the Grand National against forty other horses was quite an experience, unlike anything Joy had ever done. She said, "I'd been riding in Ireland. If I had been able to recognize the other riders and horses, it might have helped."

Joy got as far as Beecher's Brook, where she was brought down by another horse. The following year, in the open race at Aintree, she got only as far as the Chair. Third time was a charm—she rode in the Foxhunter's at Aintree, a race that makes one turn of the course rather than two, as in the Grand National itself, and made it over every fence and finished, though she can't claim to have been a factor in the race.

Joy Slater Carrier is one of three American riders, and the only woman, to successfully complete the course at Aintree and at the Maryland Hunt Cup. She is shown here aboard King Spruce in the Foxhunter's Race at Aintree in 1986. Photo: Courtesy of Joy Carrier.

Carrier said it wasn't the jumps but the large number of horses that made the Grand National so difficult. The race strategy—starting slowly and building up speed—was something different for an American, also.

Carrier, with experience in both the Grand National and the Maryland Hunt Cup, found the jumps in the latter the most difficult. At Aintree, the jumps do have a ground line and though "stiff enough for a man to walk on," have at least six inches of give to the top. The solid timber at the Maryland Hunt Cup will bring a horse down that does not clear the fence, and each fence is dead vertical, with no reassuring ground line to launch horse and rider into space. This race has its own unique pace—sometimes it is necessary to slow up, and at other spots, one should go on at a mad gallop.

Carrier was not the first woman to ride in the Grand National. That was Charlotte Brew, who rode there in 1977. Brew had already proven herself by jumping the entire course and finishing fourth in the Foxhunter's Race at Aintree in 1976. When she entered the Grand National the following year, though, she caught the full force of criticism from trainers "of the old school" and other members of the male establishment. When Jane Thorne Sloan and her twin sister, Diana Thorne Henderson, applied for their steeplechase riders' permits in England in 1976, Sloan said members of the Jockey Club asked, "You're not going to do anything silly like enter the Grand National, are you?"

Brew trailed the field in 1977, riding for a finish. The crowd applauded her over each obstacle, but unfortunately, her horse refused four from home and did not finish. It would be very rare to see a horse refuse a fence in a steeplechase under most circumstances, but it is not so unusual at the Grand National. For one thing, a horse far behind is not carried over (or knocked down at, in Carrier's case) the fearsome obstacles by a critical mass of other horses. Further, George Sloan, Jane Thorne's husband, said that sometimes horses will run all right one time, like Brew's in the Foxhunters', or in one turn of the difficult Aintree course, but lack the heart for the second circuit around. George, the only American to win the British Amateur Steeplechase Rider Championship, has tried the Grand National several times, but never finished.

Carrier's own racing career came to an end in 1987 when she received a kick in the head after falling in a race. Now she hunts, helps Rusty with his racehorses, and enjoys her show jumping, still under the masterful tutelage of Frank Chapot.

Unlike Carrier and the other women interviewed for this chapter, Blythe Miller did not start her steeplechasing career in the ladies' races. She was born at a time when she could ride straight out of the pony races into an

NSA steeplechase. Two weeks after she turned sixteen, she rode in and won her first sanctioned start in a turf race at Fair Hill, Maryland on Labor Day 1984.

In 1993, Miller came within one point of winning the Jockey Championship for the year and, in 1994, became the first woman to earn the title, which she repeated in 1995. She has racked up many more "firsts" aboard Lonesome Glory, the dominant steeplechaser horse of the 1990s.

Miller got the idea to become a jockey when as a child she, her brother Chip, Sanna Neilson, and the younger Hannums held mock steeplechases in the Cheshire hunt field. She said, "Dad was the field master, so I always sort of had to race to keep up with him, too."

When she was young, her father, steeplechase trainer Bruce Miller, raced quite a few horses at the flat track. When the children tagged along to the track, her brother Chip amused himself on the playground at Delaware Park, but Blythe studied the styles of the jockeys.

At age seventeen, Blythe wanted to be a flat jockey. She said, "I rode some at the flat track, but that's something you have to do all day—working horses in the morning and racing in the afternoon. My parents wouldn't let me miss school. I don't think that pleased me at the time, but it was probably the best thing that ever happened."

Miller finished high school and graduated from Mount Vernon College in 1992. While in college, she ran five miles a day, rode whenever she could, and started her steeplechasing career in earnest.

Between 1984 and 1988, she rode in turf races at steeplechases; then she finally got her chance over jumps. Blythe was named to ride in her first big steeplechase on May 21, 1988, and her father, always nervous before an important race, was especially rattled that day. He really wanted to win the $25,000 Mason Dixon Maiden Steeplechase, the richest race that spring for freshman jumpers. Blythe, with her limited experience, was listed as rider of Northern Pride, his carefully prepared entry. Her father fretted over his decision to use inexperienced Blythe as the minutes until starting time ticked away, but he couldn't change his mind because the other jockeys at the meet were already booked. Blythe rode Northern Pride and won the first of the many big races she has claimed.

After that, neither her father or Jonathan Sheppard, winningest steeplechase trainer in the business, were shy about giving her rides. Blythe said, "I had pretty good luck the first two years. Then it took me a few more years to get back to that level."

In 1989, Blythe qualified to ride in England after winning the American heat of the Sport of Kings Novice Challenge. She was discouraged because

Trainer Bruce Miller and his daughter, Blythe Miller, discuss strategy before a race. Photo: Betsy Branscome, The Fauquier Times-Democrat.

she wasn't very competitive in the English race, but it was obvious to those who watched her ride that her mount, the useful Jamaica Bay, just wasn't the horse for the job.

Her father was one of those watching, and with his penchant for singling out one big race to make his own, he gave the English race a lot of thought. After Jamaica Bay and other American contenders had come up short, there was a lot of discussion about whether a horse trained in America could recover from the long flight sufficiently to win the English race. Bruce Miller thought it possible and started looking for the right horse.

The right horse found him. Lonesome Glory, a big, spooky chestnut, came into his barn because the daughter of his owner, who had wanted him for a show jumper, couldn't get the horse broken. It took all the Millers and all their barn help to get the job done, and Lonesome got everyone on the ground at one time or the other in the process. In 1991, Lonesome was ready to start and won his first race that fall. He won four straight in 1992 but finished second in the first leg of the Sport of Kings when an ill-timed move by his jockey fell short. Bruce had not yet ridden his daughter on the large, difficult horse, but he put Blythe in the irons for the second leg of the race, and Lonesome won. Mrs. Walter Jeffords, his owner, wanted to try for the English races in the series and the $75,000 bonus offered if a horse could win on both sides of the Atlantic. On Dec. 12, 1992, Lonesome Glory, with Blythe in the irons, made history as the first horse trained in America to win an English hurdle race (others have won after spending the season in England with an English trainer).

Blythe's brother, Chip, observed that none of the other jockeys, who normally wish the winner well on the way back from the finish, congratulated Blythe. Women had been riding in and winning steeplechases in England since 1976, but being beaten by an American who was also a woman seemed to overcome their sense of sportsmanship.

Lonesome Glory picked up his first Eclipse award as champion steeplechaser for his efforts in 1992 and repeated in 1993 with the $250,000 Breeder's Cup Steeplechase to his credit. That was the year Blythe came within one race of capturing her first rider's title—with three wins the final day of the season.

Blythe won her first rider's championship in 1994 and repeated in 1995. Lonesome Glory was again leading steeplechase horse in 1995. Chip was nipping at her heels in 1995, but Blythe clinched the title with seven wins in the final three days of racing that year.

In 1996, Chip won the title, and Blythe finished second. Blythe's career got off to an early lead over her brother's because he was away from the horses when he went to boarding school and college. While Chip played all sports and was usually Most Valuable Player, Blythe only rode. She said, "I liked playing lacrosse, but there's only so far you can go with that."

Blythe, ever observant of such great riders as Richard Dunwoody, has always been grace itself over fences. Chip, when he started in 1990, rode more like an Indian than a stylish English rider, but his style has improved with seasoning. Blythe said, "He's strong at a fence and positive and forceful. I've always known he's better than me. He passed me in the jockey standings, but he keeps me going forward. Competition makes any sport better, and if I am beaten, I want it to be my brother who wins."

Blythe said that steeplechasing is a rough sport, especially for a woman. One particular day before the $100,000 Iroquois Steeplechase, a doctor was on hand to tape her against recent injuries so she could ride, in the same fashion that a starting quarterback would have been patched up for the

Super Bowl. At some point, she knows she will have to do something else with her life, and a continued career with horses has appeal. She said, "I'd like to train horses with my father or maybe see what I can do with some other type of riding."

Bruce Miller prefers to put the boys, rather than Blythe, on horses that are green or liable to be rough. She still gets first call on horses like Lonesome Glory, but now Chip rides as the family's stable jockey. Blythe still wins plenty of races for her father, whose charges topped the list of most purses won in 1995 and most races won in 1996, but rides first call for Jonathan Sheppard, who topped the list for most races won in 1995 and most money won in 1996.

Sheppard, an Englishman who came to this country to ride in amateur races, started training in 1966. He has been the leading trainer almost every year since, and he trains double the number of horses most trainers have in their barns. In 1995, a typical year, Sheppard had 171 starters to Bruce Miller's 53.

The first woman to ride races for Sheppard was Cathy Montgomery, who had a lot of experience on the flat track back in the days "when fans threw beer bottles at women riders," Sheppard said.

Montgomery first rode for Sheppard in 1984. Sheppard said she had more than her share of success but more than her share of injuries, also. "She was probably not quite ready for riding over fences when she started, but I'm not good about saying no." Montgomery is now Mrs. Jonathan Sheppard.

The next woman who rode for Sheppard was Blythe, his Pennsylvania neighbor and "amateur of choice" at a time when many steeplechases carded at least one race restricted to amateurs.

"Blythe has really matured as a rider. She's physically stronger and can hold horses in a race better. Her racing tactics have become more sophisticated," Sheppard said.

Currently, Sheppard's other steeplechase jockey is also a woman. Charlotte Brooks was an exercise rider and not a great one, he said. However, Sheppard gave her an opportunity to ride in a race and had a pleasant surprise.

"She didn't look very good, but in her quiet, determined way, Charlotte does very well. She's won quite a few races for me and has been darn useful. Sometimes riders are better in the afternoon than in the mornings. You just never know until you try," Sheppard said. (Note: Charlotte Brooks suffered life-threatening injuries in a race in July 1996, but through the same determination she applied to her riding, she fought her way back to health.)

Miller and Brooks aren't the only two women who ride for Sheppard. One of his favorites for his high-class flat stable is Julie Krone. He said, "Julie and Blythe are a lot alike. They're both very good about figuring horses out, especially if they have gotten to sit on the horse in the morning. They know how a horse would like to be ridden. The boys decide how they think the horse should be ridden. If the horse doesn't go along with their plan—perhaps to lay third, then win in the stretch—the boys will tell me that the horse cheated and needs a change of equipment. You'd never hear a girl say that."

Epilog

PEOPLE FOXHUNT FOR MANY REASONS. SOME GO FOR a "gallop and a gossip." I value the fellowship of the hunt field and delight in the hound work. Most of all, though, I enjoy the thrill of discovery—seeing a new vista; glimpsing a deer, hawk, or red fox; or finding a trail, gate, or jump I haven't seen before.

The sound of the huntsman's horn that got me on the scent for this book was hearing that Kathy Kusner, an Olympic rider, was almost barred from riding in the Maryland Hunt Cup. Once on the line, the quest for women who were the first in their field of riding took many unexpected turns. Some cold trails proved unproductive, and other coverts drew a blank. The quarry proved fascinating, and tales shared along the way will be long remembered and cherished.

Kathy Kusner came to an American Horse Shows Association Convention, so she was easy enough to find. Many of the other women interviewed are still in the news. Some live in the eastern United States, and some live in my home state of Virginia—a help, too. The rest are scattered to the ends of the earth, and locating them took luck.

Many attempts failed to uncover the whereabouts of Marian Coakes Mould, who still lives in England, or Penny Ann Early, believed to be in Southern California, or Norma Matthews, whose last known address was in Lexington, Kentucky and whose married name is possibly Shely.

Julie Krone rode to the top of the racing world with a win in the Belmont aboard Colonial Affair. Photo: New York Racing Association.

On this great hunt, I tracked the lives of Judy Johnson and Nancy Sweet-Escott as far as I could through magazine articles, but neither left heirs to interview. I had more luck learning about Carol Durand, who died in 1971. Her friends and relatives shared stories about her days as one of the first two women chosen to the USET jumping squad.

Sadly, three of the women who graciously shared their stories have since died: Elizabeth "Sis" Worrall, Pat Smythe, and Theodora Ayer Randolph. Their interesting lives have been much chronicled, but it is a privilege to include their last stories for posterity.

Mrs. Randolph mentioned her part in Kathy Kusner's brilliant riding career as one of her proudest moments, even above her own numerous accomplishments. It surprised me to learn that not every woman of Mrs. Randolph's day felt the same. Judy Johnson, who held a jockey's license in the 1940s, was quoted as saying that she thought the first women jockeys to follow her own example were just in it for the sensation. After women had ridden for a few years, she revised her stance to recognize that women jockeys were doing a pretty good job.

Some other women who grew up before the sexual revolution of the 1960s believed a strong man could outdo a talented woman, but even they readily admitted women could always get on with a hard-to-manage horse best because they would take the time to figure the horse out and to meet his needs with understanding, not muscle.

The most unexpected twist of all, though, was to discover that two of the women I sought out had suffered from crippling polio: Lis Hartel, the Danish dressage rider who was the first woman to win an individual medal, and Barbara Jo Rubin, the first woman to win a pari-mutuel race. In such a select group I never anticipated finding two who had to overcome the same crippling disease before riding into the record books.

Prejudice from the male hierarchy was more what I had expected to find, and I did. Jessica Newberry, whose Olympic riding career spanned twenty-eight years, with twenty-four years off to raise a family between Olympics, said some of the difficulties faced in the early days of the USET were not so much directed at women as they were organizational in nature. Still, dressage rider Marjorie Haines Gill, the first American woman to ride in the Olympics, spoke of a general feeling of malaise that emanated toward her from the male military establishment, something so subtle you could hardly put your finger on it. Diane Crump, the first woman to race on the flat track, explained that society was so ingrained in its belief in male dominance back then that she simply accepted rules barring women until Kathy Kusner took the initiative to change things.

Once women did start to ride on the flat track, signs of displeasure were anything but discreet. Bricks and bottles were heaved at the upstart women. The early women jockeys had to be escorted by security guards, partly to protect them from such violent attacks, partly to hold back the crush of equally ardent fans.

In Great Britain, treatment of women was also painfully blatant in the days before the rules changed. Women who reached the Olympic level were expected to hand over their carefully trained horses for use of the team, in the same spirit of sacrifice which had gotten the nation through the war. Women who went along, like Pat Smythe, didn't appreciate what happened to their horses as a result of the experience. Women who didn't go along, like Sheila Willcox, still vividly remember the scorn heaped upon them.

HRH Princess Anne, here enjoying the Sport of Kings Challenge at Nashville with Peter Greenall, was in 1986 the first woman to be elected president of the FEI. Photo: Jackie Burke.

The accomplishments of Sheila Willcox, and other women of her ability, finally gave rise to changes in rules to permit women to ride in the three-day at the Olympics. One of the cruel ironies is that Willcox herself was never afforded the opportunity, because even after the rule changed, the male selectors found excuses for not including her on the team. When the final vote was taken to change the rule, the British delegates voted against permitting women to ride.

Winning the right to ride in the Olympics was tricky business. Kusner and other women finally got their jockeys' licenses because those state boards denying them the right to ride were violating state and federal laws. The Olympic riding events, though, are governed by the FEI, an organization governed by delegates appointed by the participating nations. The delegates who had to rewrite the rules to include horsewomen were gentlemen of the "old school" and Old World.

Through the first half of the 20th century, the military dominated equestrian competition. As Capt. Jack Fritz said, all civilians, not just women, were 20 lengths behind military riders when cavalries were disbanded and the Olympics opened to all. Women, as in other aspects of society, were further behind than men, due to the impediment of the sidesaddle and the mores of the time.

Olympic rules softened first for women who wished to compete in dressage. "Real men," more interested in the adrenaline-accelerating sports of jumping and the three-day, lost little by conceding this point.

Women were next permitted to ride in Olympic jumping, but not before top competitors like the late Pat Smythe suffered their share of frustration on the sidelines. Kathy Kusner still keeps a letter from the USET written in response to her inquiry about trying out for the 1957 team. The person who wrote the letter said it would be unreasonable for petite Kusner to ride with as much lead as she would have to pack to make the mandatory weight of 154 pounds, and Olympic competition features "long, difficult courses over sturdy broad obstacles. Our riders must be equally strong—I doubt if you are up to that." One year before this letter was written, Pat Smythe had won the bronze medal, and women had already ridden for the USET in 1950.

Men, who put women on a pedestal during the Victorian age, really wanted to keep them there, even after women themselves complained that this was an uncomfortable and constrictive position. Men argued that women must not be permitted in sports like the three-day, racing, and steeplechasing because of the danger involved.

Almost all top female competitors have war wounds to confirm the validity of those concerns. Women riders, like men, have suffered their share of serious injuries, of career-ending falls, and for the unlucky few, death. But women have proven they are tough enough to lift themselves up from bone-jarring or bone-breaking falls to finish the course, and to rehabilitate themselves after crippling injuries in order to get back into the saddle.

Fate has whispered to Blythe Miller that someday she will have to seek another line of work. Steeplechasing is dangerous, and she realizes a woman cannot continue forever to sustain the falls that occur, on average, every eleventh race, but neither can male riders nor any other athlete continue forever.

Blythe Miller (left) and Chip Miller (second from left) strain to avoid a fallen horse and rider. Blythe is riding Strawberry Angel, sister to champion Lonesome Glory. Photo: Douglas Lees.

One begins a hunt with the preconceived notion of finding the fox. One of my premises when I started this book was that the riders I planned to interview had been born in the saddle. What I found was that many had childhoods not dissimilar to my own—they grew up in the suburbs reading horse books and dreaming of someday learning to ride and owning a horse. Kathy Kusner, Jessica Newberry Ransehousen, Sheila Willcox, Barbara Kraeling, and Ready Snodgrass all fall into this category—"late bloomers" who didn't get to start riding until they were ten or twelve.

Other women, as I had initially imagined, were born to the sport. Some of those had two riding parents and illustrious siblings as well—Jane Bullen's sister, Jennie Loriston-Clarke, represented Great Britain in dressage at the Olympics, and her brother, Michael, in the three-day; Blythe Miller's brother, Chip, claimed a Champion Steeplechase Rider's title. Joy Slater and Lana du Pont had generations of riding women to emulate. Twins Jane and Diana Thorne followed in the footsteps of their father, John Thorne, amateur steeplechase rider and breeder of fine steeplechase horses; Diana was an international-level event rider, as well. Three-day rider Caroline Treviranus Leake's parents were two of the first event riders in America.

Another category that emerged, and one that touched me, was the story of women raised in single-parent homes. Julie Krone and Pat Smythe were supported in their riding efforts by mothers who also loved horses and who made many sacrifices to give their daughters the best opportunity to succeed. Krone and Smythe have both written autobiographies in which these stories emerge.

No matter what the inclinations of the previous generations, the women interviewed proved that once the "horse bug" bites, the victim usually carries the symptoms for life and also passes it on to future generations. Almost every woman interviewed continues to have day-to-day contact with horses. Barbara Kraeling McWade and Diane Crump train race horses. Jane Bullen Holderness-Roddam runs a large training yard and serves on numerous committees of national horse organizations. Lana du Pont Wright has gone on to win the World Pairs Driving Championship and is now pursuing a third career in 100-mile endurance riding. Joy Slater Carrier foxhunts and shows jumpers. Karen Stives has become involved in the organizational side of the USET three-day team. Jessica Ransehousen served four times as chef d'equipe of the dressage team to make certain her team's van driver didn't get lost on the way to the Olympic competition, as her own did in Rome.

The list goes on. Gold medalist Liselott Linsenhoff is the mother of Ann-Katrin Linsenhoff, herself a winner of the team dressage gold medal at the 1988 Olympics. Mary Mairs and Frank Chapot are parents of Laura, who rides jumpers on the grand prix level, just as her mother and father did, and Wendy, who rides amateur jumpers. Ransehousen's daughter, Missy, and Lana Wright's daughter, Beale, both ride upper-level three-day. Katrina Gifford appears destined to ride on the British three-day team. Her mother Althea Rogers-Smith rode for the British show jumping team when women were still a novelty in international competition, and her father is leading English steeplechase trainer Josh Gifford. Kassie Kingsley and her former husband Arch, himself once an active point-to-point rider, are the parents of Arch and George, both winning on the steeplechase circuit. Mrs. Theo Randolph's daughter, Nina Bonnie, annually tops the list of amateur-owner hunter riders. Mrs. Nancy Hannum's son, Buzz, won the Maryland Hunt Cup twice, and grandson, Buck Davidson, is following the path of his gold medal–winning father, Bruce, into the upper level of the three-day. Patty Barton, one of the most successful of the early women jockeys, is mother of Donna Barton, exercise girl for D. Wayne Lukas (currently racing's winningest trainer) and on her own climb to fame as a jockey.

Blythe Miller and Julie Krone signaled the end of the long run. My brief conversation with Jonathan Sheppard had the same effect as hearing the huntsman blow "going home" on his horn. I knew it was time to head for the van and put this horse (book) to bed.

Jonathan Sheppard employs Julie Krone and Blythe Miller, not in response to affirmative action, but because he wants to win races and make money. Blythe Miller rode winners of an incredible $596,871 in 1995, the second highest total ever garnered by a steeplechase rider. Krone has won over $53 million in purses, and this figure climbs at a rate of about two stakes races per week.

A woman born after 1968 can't conceive of being barred from riding in any competition for which one is qualified. That was the year that Kusner and Audrey Melbourne proved once and for all that women had the legal right to hold a jockey's license, thus clearing the track for Krone, Miller, and every other young girl who has ever wanted to ride a racehorse.

Krone can't even remember a time when her sex counted against her in her career as a jockey, though admits it may have once been a factor. Miller couldn't comprehend the concept of being restricted to riding only in ladies' races.

The financial successes of Miller and Krone are heartening. Women jockeys who preceded them made ends meet by bunking in the tack room, washing dishes in diners, and often galloping more than eighteen horses per day. Even Krone boarded with relatives, then with her agent's family, early in her career.

Miller and Krone have the right to continue their careers as jockeys as long as physically able; in fact, they have the right to pursue their chosen careers at all, because of the efforts of the women interviewed for this book. The women who broke the barriers in each aspect of competition generously shared their stories, and their tales of trial and triumph will not be forgotten.

The stories I will remember sitting by the fire after the long hunt are ones of courage, as I would have expected, but not just physical courage. It was the moral courage and belief in one's self that were so inspiring. None of the women who brought about change suggested they had gone through the rigors for the good of the society. They acted through the belief that they were good enough to be given a chance to ride at the very highest levels without restrictions. The next time I hesitate before plunging into uncharted waters, I shall try to remember Kathy Kusner's simple philosophy: "If I want to do something, and I'm not doing it now, what have I got to lose by trying?"

In retrospect, all can see that the women, while acting for themselves, did clear the stones from the path for the young women riders of today. Diane Crump said she wouldn't be comfortable for her own daughter, Della, now seventeen, to go off to the race track right after graduating from high school as she did. She said of her own travels into the world at such a tender age, "Maybe my parents and I were naive, or maybe the world was a more innocent place back then, but I hope Della will find what, in her heart, she wants to do and do it with the passion I have felt for my riding through all these years."

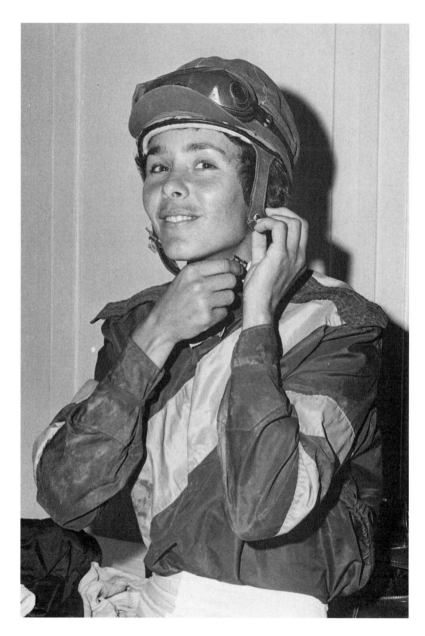

Kathy Kusner, before a race at Charles Town. Photo: Courtesy of Kathy Kusner.

Bibliography

Acton, Lucy. "Judy Johnson Remembers." *The Maryland Horse.* November, 1977.

Alcock, Anne. *"They're Off!" The Story of the First Girl Jump Jockeys.* London: J.A. Allen, 1978.

American Horse Shows Association. *Official Horse Show Records.* American Horse Shows Association, 1934, 1935, 1936.

Apsley, Lady. *Bridleways Through History.* London: Hutchinson Ltd., 1936.

Armstrong, Virginia Winmill Livingstone. *"Gone Away" With the Winmills.* Warwickshire, Eng.: Tomes of Leamington, 1977.

Beach, Belle. *Riding and Driving for Women.* New York: Charles Scribner's Sons, 1912.

Braudel, F. *The Structures of Everyday Life,* Vol. I. New York: Harper & Row, 1981.

Briggs, Asa. *A Social History of England.* New York: Viking Press, 1983.

Browne, Capt. T.H. *A History of the English Turf.* New York: Scribner's, 1931.

Bumgartner, Frederic J. *Henry II, King of France 1547-1559.* Durham, N.C.: Duke University Press, 1988.

Buxton, Meriel. *Ladies of the Chase.* London: The Sportsman's Press, 1987.

Chenevix-Trench, Charles. *A History of Horsemanship.* Garden City, N.Y.: Doubleday & Co., Inc., 1970.

Colgan, Charles T., and Gallo Jr., William. *American Steeplechasing.* Elmont, N.Y.: National Steeplechase and Hunt Association, 1980, 1982, 1983. Elkton, Md: National Steeplechase Association, 1993, 1994.

Cooper, John E. *Steeplechasing in America.* Elmont, N.Y.: Triangle Publications, 1969.

D'Este, Carlo. *Patton, A Genius for War.* New York: Harper Collins, 1995.

Dillon, Jane Marshall. *School for Young Riders.* New York: D. Van Nostrand Co., 1958.

F.E.I. *General Regulations of the Fédération Equestre Internationale.* 10th ed. Brussels: Fédération Equestre Internationale, 1957.

F.E.I. *Rules for Competition in the Open—Three-Day Events.* 11th ed. Brussels: Fédération Equestre Internationale, 1963.

F.E.I. *Statutes General Regulations of the Fédération Equestre Internationale Olympic Games.* 6th ed. Brussels: Fédération Equestre Internationale, 1938. 9th ed., 1953.

Fleitmann-Bloodgood, Lida L. *Saddle of Queens.* London: J.A. Allen, 1959.

Foster, Carol. *Badminton Horse Trials.* London: Barrie & Jenkins, 1980.

Fraser, Antonia. *The Weaker Vessel.* New York: Alfred A. Knopf, 1984.

Freeman, G.W. *The Masters of Eventing.* New York: Arco Publishing Co., 1978.

Freeman, Margaret C. "Road to Atlanta." *The Chronicle of the Horse.* Anne Kursinski, May 10, 1996. Dorothy Trapp, May 24, 1996.

Goldstein, Jane. "Judy Johnson." *The Blood-Horse.* Feb. 8, 1971.

Grace, Art. "Race Is Long in First Ride," *The Blood-Horse,* Feb. 15, 1969.

Greenberg, Stan. *Guinness Book of the Olympics.* Middlesex, Eng.: Enfield, 1983.

Grombach, John V. *1972 Olympic Guide.* New York: Coronet Communications, 1972.

Haight, Walter. "Forward Pass 7-5 To Win Preakness." *Washington Post.* May 17, 1968.

Haney, Lynn. *The Lady Is a Jockey.* New York: Dodd, Mead and Co., 1973.

Harper, Harriet Wadsworth. *Around the World in Eighty Years on a Sidesaddle.* New York: The Spiral Press, 1966.

Hibbert, Christopher. *The English, A Social History,* 1066-1945. New York: W.W. Norton & Co., 1987.

Hickey, Joe. "Judy Johnson." *The Maryland Horse,* September 1968, p. 60-65.

Hollingsworth, Kent. "What's Going on Here," *The Blood-Horse,* Dec. 9, 1967; Oct. 5, 1968; May 3, 1969.

Howard, Donald R. *Chaucer, His Life, His Works, His World.* New York: E.P. Dutton, 1987.

Hutchison, Harold F. *The Hollow Crown: A Life of Richard II.* New York: John Day Co., 1961.

Jaffer, Nancy, ed. *Riding for America.* New York: Doubleday, 1990.

Kennedy, Art. "Women Jockeys Kill the Notion," *Spur of Virginia*. Winter, 1973.

Kneeland, Charlotte Brailey. *Side-saddle Riding for Beginners*. Alton Bay, N.H.: Yesteryear Publishing Co., 1994.

Krone, Julie. *Riding for My Life*. New York: Little, Brown and Co., 1995.

L'Année Hippique, 1952-53, pp. 54-56, 39-40; 1972-73, pp. 39-42.

Liss, Peggy K. *Isabel the Queen: Life and Times*. New York: Oxford University Press, 1992.

Los Deportes Ecuestres in Los Juegos de la XIX Olimpiada.

Martin, Ann. *The Equestrian Woman*. New York: Paddington Press, 1979.

Maryland Horse, The. "Judy Johnson to Run Blarney." July, 1963.

_____. "Miss Kusner Gets License." November, 1968.

_____. "Obituaries—Judy Johnson." November, 1978.

Master of Foxhounds Association of America. Boston: 1923, 1928, 1931, 1935, 1955. Leesburg, Va.: 1994-95.

Mathew, Gervase. *The Court of Richard II*. London: Murray, 1968.

Neale, John Ernest. *The Age of Catherine de' Medici*. London: Jonathan Cape, 1957.

Newsum, Gillian. *Women & Horses*. New York: Howell Book House, 1988.

O'Connor, Sally, ed. *The USCTA Book of Eventing*. Reading, Mass: Addison-Wesley Publishing Co., Inc., 1982.

Perrone, Vinnie. "Crushing Fall Can't Bend Her Will: After Painful Recovery, Krone to Resume Race-Riding Next Week." *Washington Post*. May 12, 1994.

Pollitt, J.J. *Art and Experience in Classical Greece*. Cambridge: Cambridge University Press, 1972.

Potter, David. *A History of France, 1460-1560: The Emergence of a Nation State*. New York: St. Martin's Press, 1995.

Prescott, William Hickling. *Prescott's Ferdinand and Isabella*. New York: Heritage Press, 1962 (first published in 1837).

Roeder, Ralph. *Catherine de' Medici and the Lost Revolution*. New York: The Viking Press, 1937.

Rossell, John E. *The Maryland Hunt Cup, Past and Present*. Baltimore: The Sporting Press, 1975.

Silver, Caroline. *Eventing, The Classic Equestrian Sport*. New York: St. Martin's Press, Inc., 1977.

Smythe, Pat. *Jump for Joy*. New York: A.S. Barnes & Co., 1955.

_____. *One Jump Ahead*. New York: A.S. Barnes & Co., 1957.

_____. *Show Jumping*. Cranbury, N.J.: A.S. Barnes and Co., 1968.

Sprague, Kurth. *The National Horse Show, A Centennial History 1883-1983.* New York: National Horse Show Foundation, 1985.

Steinkraus, William C., and Savitt, Sam. *Great Horses of the United States Equestrian Team.* New York: Dodd, Mead & Co., 1977.

Steinkraus, William C., ed. *The U.S. Equestrian Team Book of Riding.* New York: Simon and Schuster, 1976.

Stratton, Charles. *Encyclopaedia of Show Jumping.* London: Robert Hale, 1973.

Surtees, R.S. "Ask Mamma"; or, *The Richest Commoner in England.* London: Bradbury Agnew & Co., 1858.

Surtees, R.S. *Mr. Sponge's Sporting Tour.* London: Bradbury Agnew & Co., 1852.

Sweet-Ascot, Nancy. *The Clergyman's Daughter, Memoirs of Nancy Sweet-Ascot.* Wilmington, Del.: Serendipity Press, 1984.

de Trannoy, General Baron. *Jeux Equestris de a XVI Olympiade Grand Prix de Dressage.* Brussels: Fédération Equestre Internationale, 1956.

Trollope, Anthony. *Hunting Sketches.* New York: John Day, 1953. (First published in 1865.)

Van Urk, J. Blan. *The Story of American Foxhunting,* Vol. 1. New York: The Derrydale Press, 1940.

Wathen, Guy. *Great Horsemen of the World.* North Pomfret, Vt.: Trafalgar Square Publishing, 1991.

Welcome, John. *The Sporting Empress, The Story of Elizabeth of Austria and Bay Middleton.* London: Michael Joseph, 1975.

Willcox, Sheila. *The Event Horse.* London: Pelham Books Ltd., 1973.

Winants, Peter, ed. *American Gold, The Story of the Equestrian Sports of the 1984 Olympics.* Middleburg, Va.: The Chronicle of the Horse, 1984.

Winants, Peter. "The Saga of Chase Me." *The Chronicle of the Horse,* Oct. 27, 1972, pp. 7-8.

Yorke, Tom. "A Landmark Decision." *Horse Digest,* Nov. 1982.

INDEX

Aitcheson, Joe, 133, 134, 167
American Horse Shows Association, 17, 40, 41, 95, 97, 171
Andersen, Gunther, 68
Anne of Beaujeu, 28–29
Anne of Bohemia, 12
Anne, Princess (of England), 103, 104, 122, 184
Anne, Queen (of England), 31
Antoinette, Marie, 15
Apsley, Lady, 26
Artemis, 27
Atkinson, Mrs. Neville Lemmon, 19
Ayer, Neil, 125

Badminton Horse Trials, 106–9, 110, 111, 113, 119, 123, 124
Barton, Donna, 153, 188
Barton, Patty, 153, 188
Baucher, François, 16
Baxter, Ellie Wood Keith, 84, 86
Beach, Belle, 26
Beach, Tom, 166, 168, 169
Beach, Virginia, 169
Belmont Stakes, 47, 155
Beaufort, Duke of, 106, 107
Bird, Betty Bosley, 7–8, 53–54, 56, 84
Bloodgood, Lida Fleitmann, 16

Bonnie, Nina, 38, 40, 188
Borg, Robert, 63, 66, 72
Bosley, Elizabeth. See Bird, Betty Bosley
Bosley, Elizabeth Cromwell, 54–56
Boyce, Joan, 84, 168
Breeder's Cup Steeplechase, 178
Brew, Charlotte, 175
British Jockey Club, 49, 142, 175
Brooks, Charlotte, 179, 180
Bullen, Jane, 7, 103, 112, 123–25, 187
Burghley Horse Trials, 110, 111, 112, 123, 124, 127
Burr, Leslie, 98, 99
Burton, Jonathan, 114–15
Butcher, Susan, 8

Calder. See Tropical Park
Cancre, Michele, 79
Caprilli, Federico, 26
Carrier, Joy, 170–75, 187
Cassell, Patti, 166
Catherine the Great, 15
Cavalry, 63, 82, 85, 92–93, 104, 106, 114, 185
Chapot, Frank, 96, 98, 132, 171, 187
Chapot, Laura, 96, 187
Chapot, Mary. See Mairs, Mary
Charles Town Races, 134, 152–53

195

Chatfield-Taylor, Katherine. *See* Kingsley, Katherine
Christmas, Billy, 157, 158
Churchill Downs, 145, 149, 156
Clark, Stephen, 26, 52–53
Coakes, Marion, 94, 95, 181
Cook Foundation, Marjorie, 136
Cotter, Margaret, 83, 84
Coulthard, Elisabeth, 84
Crump, Diane, 149–52, 154, 156, 183, 187, 189

Davidson, Bruce, 127–28, 130, 188
Dawson, Phyllis, 130
Dean, Mrs. Archie, 62, 73
De Poitiers, Diane, 15
Diana, 27
Dillon, Jane Marshall, 91
Divine, Don, 149
Dressage, 6, 8, 57–74, 114, 120, 127
Drummond-Hay, Jane, 107
Du Pont, Jean, 84
Du Pont, Lana, 6, 101, 103, 111, 119–23, 187, 188
Du Pont, Mrs. Richard, 119
Durand, Carol, 85, 87–90, 182

Early, Penny Ann, 143, 145–46, 147, 149, 181
Eclipse Award, 141, 178
Elizabeth I, 31
Elizabeth, Empress (of Austria), 33–34
English Enclosure Acts, 16, 29
Epona, 27
Eventing, 6–8, 28, 101–30

Fanning, Jill, 170–71, 172
Fargis, Joe, 91, 98
Fédération Equestre International (FEI), 60–61, 68, 75–76, 78–79, 82, 87, 88, 89, 111, 117, 124, 184, 185
Fillis, James, 69
Florida State Racing Commission, 147, 148, 149
Forbes, John, 157–58
Foxcroft School, 39
Freeman, Kevin, 120, 121, 125, 127
Fritz, Jack, 85, 185
Furness, Elizabeth Merrill, 17, 18, 20, 35, 41

Galvin, Patricia, 70–73
Gifford, Mrs. Josh. *See* Rogers-Smith, Althea
Gill, Marjorie Haines, 61–66, 69, 183
Gordon-Watson, Mary, 124
Grand National Steeplechase, 1, 173–75
Grand-prix jumping, 1, 5, 8, 25, 66, 74, 75–100
Grant, Chuck, 155

Gulfstream Park, 149, 151
Gurney, Hilda, 72

Hannum, Nancy Penn-Smith, 37–39, 128, 163–64, 188
Harjes, Joan, 117
Harper, Mrs. Fletcher, 17, 18
Hartel, Lis, 6, 66–70, 183
Harts, Catherine, 21–23
Hatherley, Sue, 103
Henderson, Mrs. Nick. *See* Thorne, Diana
Henneberg, Jill, 130
Hialeah Park, 149, 152
Hirsch, Mary, 48, 55, 56
Hirsch, Mary Ryan. *See* Ryan, Mary
Hirsch, Max, 48, 54–55
Hirsch, Mrs. Bill. *See* Ryan, Mary
Hodgson, Janet, 103
Hofmann, Carol, 94
Holderness-Roddam, Jane. *See* Bullen, Jane
Horse shows, 9–10, 17, 21, 22, 26, 41, 45
Horton, Sandra, 142
Hough, Margaret, 107
Hoyer, Sandra, 17
Hugo-Vidal, Victor, 69–70
Hulbert, William P., 21–22, 23
Hunting, 11, 14–15, 16–20, 22, 23–24, 26–43, 45

Iditarod, 8
International Sidesaddle Organization (of Spain), 17
Isabella, Queen, 13, 28

Jacquin, Lisa, 100
Japanese horse racing, 158–59
Jockey's Guild, 137, 148–49
Johnsey, Debbie, 96
Johnson, Judy, 45–49, 52, 182–83

Kees, Barbara, 50–51
Keim, Mary, 149
Keith, Mrs. Julian, 33
Kellett, Iris, 171
Kentucky Derby, 149
Kentucky Racing Commission, 143, 147
Kingsley, Arch, 165, 188
Kingsley, George, 165, 188
Kingsley, Katherine, 163, 164–66, 188
Kraeling, Barbara, 7, 168–70, 187
Krone, Julie, 154–59, 180, 182, 187, 188–89
Kuckluk, Herbert, 70
Kursinski, Anne, 98, 100
Kusner, Kathy, 1–3, 5, 25, 41, 42, 77, 78, 90–94, 96, 131–43, 145, 147, 152, 153,

157, 159, 161–63, 181, 183, 185, 187, 188

LaFond, Leonard, 71–72
Lake Magdalene Farm, 151–52
Lang, Chick Jr., 157
Leaping head, 16
LeGoff, Jack, 125–28, 130
Lende, Karen, 130
Leng, Virginia, 130
Linsenhoff, Liselott, 7, 70, 71, 187
Litchfield, Mary, 92
Littauer, Vladimir, 91
Lorriston-Clark, Jennie, 123, 187
Louis XV, 15

Machin-Goodall, Vivian, 106
Mahieu, Janine, 79
Mairs, Mary, 94–96, 187
Marie Antoinette, 15
Marjorie Cook Foundation, 136
Mary II, 31
Maryland Hunt Cup, 1–2, 5, 53–54,
    161–63, 171, 173, 175
Maryland Racing Commission, 48, 50, 52,
    134, 136–38, 147, 163
Maryland State Court, 138, 143
Mason, Diana, 107
Master of Foxhounds Association, 36, 37
Matthews, Norma, 85, 87, 88, 89–90, 181
McCashin, Arthur, 87–89
McDonald, Mrs. John, 84
McIntosh, Karen, 62
McKinney, Rigan, 52, 137
McKnight, Elizabeth, 172
McKnight, Turney, 162, 172
McWade, Barbara. *See* Kraeling, Barbara
Medici, Catherine de, 13–15, 16, 28, 29
Melbourne, Audrey, 134–139, 188
Mellon, Paul, 12, 14, 28, 30, 32, 40, 46, 166
Middleburg races. *See* Virginia Spring
    Steeplechase
Middleton, Bay, 33
Miller, Blythe, 175–80, 186, 187, 188–89
Miller, Bruce, 176, 177, 179
Miller, Chip, 176, 178, 179, 186, 187
Monahan-Prudent, Katie, 97
Monk, Donnan Sharp, 59, 73, 101, 119–21
Montgomery, Cathy, 179
Moore, Anne, 94
Morganthau, Joan, 4, 5
Morkis, Dorothy, 72
Morris, Col. Howard, 5
Morris, George, 93, 94, 97
Moss, Virginia, 50
Mott, Thomas T., 46, 47

Mould, Marion. *See* Coakes, Marion
Murdock, Margaret, 8–9
Murphy, Dennis, 5

Nagle, Florence, 49
National Steeplechase and Hunt Association.
    See National Steeplechase Association
National Steeplechase Association (NSA),
    139, 163, 166, 168, 170, 176
Naughton, Muriel, 142
Neilson, Sanna, 173, 176
Neilson, Toinette. *See* Phillips, Toinette
Nemethy, Bertalan de, 92–93, 96, 98, 157
Newberry, Jessica, 63, 68. *See also*
    Ransehousen, Jessica Newberry
Newman, Kathy Doyle, 173
National Horse Show (New York), 66, 84
New York Racing Association, 45, 48, 56
Noland, Charlotte, 39

O'Connor, Karen. *See* Lende, Karen
O'Shea, Joan, 145

Pace, Jerry, 156
Page, Michael, 70, 120, 125
Patton, Gen. George, 59–60, 62
Pellier, Atelier, 16
Perkins, Beth, 127
Perry, Betty, 84
Phillips, Toinette, 168, 170
Picou, Clarence, 156
Pillion, 11
Pimlico Race Course, 52, 151
Plumb, Donnan. *See* Monk, Donnan Sharp
Plumb, Michael, 120, 125, 126, 127, 128
Poe, Albert, 40, 41
Pony Club, 3, 5, 6, 115, 116, 123, 127
Potts, Gertrude Rives, 36–37
Prior-Palmer, Lucinda, 103, 111, 124
Proctor, Tom, 145, 146
Proctor, Willard, 145, 146

Racing, 8, 45–56, 131–59
Rall, Vivian, 168
Randolph, A.C., 40–42, 91–92
Randolph, Theodora Ayer, 35, 38–43, 132,
    182, 188
Ransehousen, Jessica Newberry, 63–64, 70,
    72–74, 183, 187, 188
Richards, Joseph III, 47, 48
Riflery, 8–9
Rivett-Carnac, Frances Clytie, 8
Robbiani, Heidi, 98
Roberts, Emmett, 52
Robinson, Penny, 5
Rochester, Elizabeth, 117–18

Rogers-Smith, Althea, 188
Roszel, Sally, 51–53, 56
Roycroft, Bill, 101, 125
Rubin, Barbara Jo, 139, 146–49, 152–54, 183
Rudd, Terry, 97
Ruhsam, Joey, 168, 170
Ryan, Mary, 139, 140, 163, 166, 167–68

Sailing, 8
St. Cyr, Henri, 71
Salisbury, Marchioness of, 29
Schockaert, Brigitte, 5, 79
Scott, Marion du Pont, 84
Sears, Marie, 21
Secor, Sarah Bosley, 8, 54–56
Serrell, Margarita, 68, 72–73
Sexton, Sallie, 41
Sharp, Donnan. See Monk, Donnan Sharp
Sheppard, Jonathan, 176, 179–80, 188
Show jumping, 5, 8, 9
Sidesaddle, 8, 10, 11–26, 31, 34, 84
Skinner, Jack, 23, 52
Skinner, Mildred, 23–26
Slater, Jill. See Fanning, Jill
Slater, Joy. See Carrier, Joy
Sloan, George, 175
Sloan, Jane Thorne, 9, 141, 142, 144, 167, 175, 187
Smith, Melanie, 96–100
Smith, Mignon C., 5
Smithwick, D.M. "Mikey," 54, 132, 134, 136, 137, 161, 164
Smythe, Pat, 5, 6, 76, 78–82, 90, 182, 183, 185, 187
Snodgrass, Ready, 163, 166–67, 187
Sport of Kings Steeplechase, 176–78
Stecken, Fritz, 61–64, 66, 69
Steeplechase, 7, 8, 9, 41, 45, 47, 48, 52, 161–80
Steinkraus, William C., 87, 89, 90, 96, 100, 137
Steinman, Peggy, 84
Stickley, Lovell, 169
Stives, Karen, 128, 129, 187
Stuckelberger, Christine, 58
Sunshine Park, 151, 152
Sutton, Ann, 130
Sweet-Escott, Nancy, 49–50, 182

Tampa Bay Downs, 156, 158. See also Sunshine Park
Tauskey, Mary Anne, 127–28
Taylor, Ann Hardaway. See Sutton, Ann

Thompson, Carol, 120
Thorne, Diana, 142, 175, 187
Thorne, Jane. See Sloan, Jane Thorne
Three-day. See Eventing
Thuss, Pat, 5
Tippett, Liz Whitney, 84, 85
Treviranus, Caroline, 102, 127–28, 187
Treviranus, Stewart, 113–14, 117, 118–19, 127
Trollope, Anthony, 32–33
Tropical Park, 146, 147–48

United States Combined Training Association (USCTA), 102, 125, 128
United States Equestrian Team (USET), 59, 62–64, 72, 73, 85, 87, 89, 90, 91, 92–94, 97, 114, 117, 118, 125, 132, 137, 157, 171, 182, 185, 187
United States Olympic Organizing Committee, 134
Uphoff, Nicole, 71

Valentine, Mrs. Miles, 170, 172
Victoria, Queen (of England), 32, 33
Virginia Gold Cup, 166–67, 173
Virginia Spring Steeplechase (at Middleburg), 163, 164, 166

Waller, Mrs. Thomas, 84
Walsh, Joan, 84
Walton, Jil, 130
Ward, Bettina, 40
Warden, Margaret Lindsley, 115, 116
Watjen, Richard, 62, 120
Watkins, Torrence, 126, 128
Watt, Elaine Shirley, 69–70
Webb, Bryan, 146, 147, 152
Wheeler, Sally, 84
Wight, Harry, 164, 166
Willcox, Sheila, 107–13, 124, 183, 185, 187
Wilmot, Norah, 49
Winmill, Viola, 36
Wofford, Dawn Palethorpe, 82
Wofford, J.E.B., 82, 118
Wofford, Jimmy, 62, 63, 128
Wofford, John W., 62
World War II, 10, 37, 48, 49, 59, 63, 75, 92
Worrall, Elizabeth "Sis," 17, 18, 21, 182
Wright, Beale, 123
Wright, Gordon, 63, 73
Wright, Mrs. W.C. See Du Pont, Lana

Equal to the challenge : pioneering women of
798 BUR   00046994

Burke, Jackie C.
